BETRAYED
and
BETRAYER

Ben Wilson
and
Ann Wilson

BETRAYED
and
BETRAYER

Copyright © 2015 Ben and Ann Wilson

Paperback ISBN: 978-0-692-41405-7

Printed in the United States of America

DEDICATION

This book is dedicated to Larry Crabb.

Thanks for helping a generation live more authentically and dependent on Christ.

ACKNOWLEDGEMENTS

We want to thank the following folks for their influence in our lives, help on our journey and support for this project:

Our parents, Ron and Judy Wilson, and Carl and Betty Morris, Thad Wilson for introducing us, Stephanie Wilson, Payne Wilson, Nora Sherrill, Brad and Jenn Dugan, Chuck and Susanne Roberts, Donald and Bonnie Morris, Michael and Sara Garcia, Karen Blakeman, Dave and Laura White, Barb Hill, Norm and Lisa Wilkinson, Tonia and Marlin Parrott, Mike and Cathy Misko, Tamra and Daniel Dougherty, Brett and Keli Daily, Rob and Corie Schoeneberg, Krista and Nick Brennfoerder, KC and Kinsey Maddox, Joe and Erin Montgomery, Tessia and Keith Reeves, Stan and Elayna Utley, Becky Gonzales, Keith and Karen Cowling, Terry and Theresa Mullins, Lillian-Grace Misko, Julianne Thompson, Tania McGregor, Myko Milstien, Christine and Jack Rogers, Julie and Steve Alley, Kathy Ramser, Dani Combs, Emily Russell, Allison and Ernie Givens, Bart Wilson, Melinda Nguyen, Pam Pedrow and the gang at The Counseling Center at Calvary, Chris English, Katie Randolph, Shaun and Cat Germain, Tara Mayberry, Brad Woods, Sherri Stiles, Kim Case, Kristen Shadden, Gary Hassani, Tom Varney, Aram and Ellen Haroutunian, Steve and Pam Smallwood, Sammie the lab, our CCU classmates and community, Matt Shetley, Jill Szoo Wilson, Michael Cusick, Wes and Judy Roberts, Larry Crabb, Jennifer

Clark, Michael Klassen, Tom Freiling, John Carrington and Jaylyn Gough.

Our hearts are full of gratitude for each of you.

CONTENTS

CONTENTS

DANCING WITH GOD

BEN

2014 marked the 20th anniversary of the revelation of my wife's affair. The day I found out about her affair was the best day of my life because that's when I woke up as a man. It was the worst day of my life because of the intense pain and trauma. Facing our pain, sorrow and grief was worth it a thousand times over. We survived the Mad Max journey of affair recovery and now help restore and rebuild other marriages.

Ten years post affair, Ann and I hosted a party to celebrate the snatching of victory from the jaws of defeat. We celebrated God choosing us while we are at our worst as one victory, and we commemorated the thrill of being happily together after traversing through tons of shite together as another.

As I prepared for the event, I spoke to a friend and mentioned the celebration barbecue we were hosting. "This Labor Day marks ten years since I learned of her affair. We began living honestly that day or honestly living that day." I said. "We're celebrating the ten-year anniversary of the best and worst day of our lives."

Caught off guard, he said, "What do you want to do that for?"

With a wry smile, I explained how I wanted to dance on the place of my worst pain. I referred to a truth; I also referenced words of an author he and I respect who encourages abuse victims to envision doing just that – dancing on their worst pain. I said, "I want to dance a dance of redemption over the moment that nearly shattered everything for my bride and me."

At the risk of sounding like the Saturday Night Live Church Lady, I then said, "I want to dance with God on Satan's neck."

Here we are, years later, and my goodness, I love Ann. She is lovely. I don't ever want to lose her. Together, we respond to a calling we understand is just plain weird to many folks. Most people I know aren't talking about their affairs or most painful moments decades later in any great detail. But that is what we do.

Our redemptive story generally blesses couples dealing with an affair. Sometimes we hear from naysayers who want us to quit talking about the affair, but that won't happen any time soon by our choice. We hear accusations of not being past the affair because we share with fresh pain. We stay in touch with our pain to first help us remember the great loss and pain infidelity brings so we don't repeat it, and secondly to share authentically a first-person account with real emotions and not in a detached third-person manner.

This book is gritty. These pages contain our pain, our anger and the messiness an affair creates. It also contains the redemptive power of surrendering our story to the One who heals. Our experience demonstrates that an affair doesn't necessarily signal the end of your marriage. Within these pages, there is hope, grace and an invitation from us and God to dance on Satan's neck as we did at our celebration barbeque.

We invite you to celebrate with us. Right now you may not feel like celebrating. Our guess is that since you've opened this book an affair by either you or your mate is now part of your journey. This is a painful, confusing time. You may not know which way is up. We hope you are encouraged (en-*courage*-ed) on your journey of healing and someday we can celebrate with you.

In *Betrayed and Betrayer,* you will find direction. We'll share reflections, some heavy and some light, about our own journey and practical information to help you survive the initial 30 days of chaotic emotions following the revelation of an affair. We'll guide you through the twists and turns of the first 90 days and all the while provide a road map for the growth of your relationship and restoration of your marriage.

Some days you may be overwhelmed and throw this book across the room. That's okay. (If you're reading in eBook format you might not want to throw it.) Muster the courage to pick it back up and keep reading even when the pain is intense. On this journey, you will experience hopelessness. But remember, hopeless isn't the final word. Borrow our hope as you read and know that we experienced hopelessness on the way, too. By consistently staying with the process we made the journey from hard to hope and ultimately to a close, passionate marriage that inspires others.

Much Grace,
Ben and Ann

AS YOU BEGIN

BEN AND ANN

*L*ike a travel journal, this book chronicles our journey. *Betrayed and Betrayer* will help you navigate your journey through betrayal with reflections and practical guidance. Your journey is no doubt different from ours, so as you read look for bigger themes in our words, and don't get bogged down in the details especially if your betrayal story seems vastly different.

We recommend you read through the book in its entirety over a couple of days, and then go back and read a reflection daily. We are aware you may skip around the book to look for certain topics. That's okay. Most of the reflections stand on their own.

This book includes coarse and raw language. Affair recovery isn't G-rated. We reflect the depth and passion of the process especially in our story, the two reflections on *The King's Speech* movie and in the final reflection. We hope the language won't distract you from the deeper messages of this book but we felt it important to be authentic. This book also includes certain words that are capitalized as coming from God, such as Grace, Love, Freedom. These refer to a bigger reality than our own.

Speaking of movies, we didn't intend to write a book with so many movie clips, but scenes from movies help bypass our rational defenses by engaging our imagination, longings and emotions. When we share a movie clip in a reflection, even if you haven't seen the movie, we hope you connect with the theme illustrated by the clip.

Both of you are extremely vulnerable right now. You'll be tempted to relieve the pain in unhealthy ways that will cause more damage to your relationship. Avoid big decisions like getting even, changing jobs, moving or significant financial expenditures. To avoid contact with the affair partner, one or more of these may be necessary, but wait for clarity down the road.

Be honest. Disclose everything. One mistake betrayers make is to gradually disclose painful truths. It's best to reveal the whole truth in one sitting, although specific sexual details may not be helpful (sexual details create images that are tough to erase later on). If you remember more general details, share those as you remember. Honesty is essential to the healing path. Honesty helps you move through the pain. Honesty may bring more pain in the moment yet provides the greatest chance of completing the journey.

Be aware that this messy process lasts longer than you expect given the influence of our microwave society. Stay engaged with the process, especially when your insides are screaming "run away" because it is too painful. This takes courage, but you have more courage than you know.

The late Rich Mullins sang, "Even if I made my bed in Hell, still there you would find me, 'cause nothing is beyond you." This perilous journey is bigger than you. It is beyond you but not beyond Him. Be open to God's pursuit and the mystery of it all.

OUR STORY

ANN

"*Y*ou fuckin' whore!"

These were Ben's first words after I told him about my affair.

Fast-forward 20 years. Now when people ask me about my marriage, I frequently paraphrase a Winnie the Pooh quote. "If Ben lives to be a hundred, I want to live to be a hundred minus one day so I never have to live a day without him."

Today, our marriage is great - not perfect but really great. We've developed a beautiful rhythm. Ben cherishes me, my soul. I am more aware of his soul, his grief and his joy. Not that we don't occasionally miss each other's hearts. We are human. It happens. But we talk it through and regain our rhythm much more quickly than before.

We hang out on our red leather sofa or around a crackling firepit in our backyard. We enjoy being adventurous, from new culinary attempts to traveling halfway around the world with friends to counsel missionaries.

Ben completed his first Ironman last year and keeps me from drowning as I train for my first triathlon. We are silly with each other. I enjoy Ben's quick wit, and I delight in his humor.

A co-worker once told me I wouldn't understand her impending divorce because I had such a great marriage. I told her it wasn't always so. She looked stunned as I told her of our journey. We went from an unhealthy dating relationship (we thought we were fine at the time), through the years of denial and my affair, to healing years of searing pain and honesty with our own stories, with each other and with God. The marriage she sees today reflects love, respect, tenderness, laughter, life, light, grace and growth.

How does a couple go from screaming cuss words to tender devotion after an affair?

It's hard.

So let's back up.

As a high school senior, I walked out of Kwik Check, the local convenience store, and heard someone say, "Hey girl, can you tell me where Thad Wilson lives?" I direct Ben and his college friend to Thad's house and go on to meet my date for the evening. Our relationship began. Pretty classy, eh? Not so much. Providence was at work that night, because if I had walked out five seconds sooner or five seconds later, this book would not be in your hands right now.

That fall, I attended the same college as Ben and his friend. Ben and I had exchanged letters over the summer, and he was so smitten that he left a note on my dorm room door the day I arrived. In fact, as I called the number on the note a knock interrupted the call. I opened the door to a tall, handsome guy with great hair in white shorts, red t-shirt and dark legs from continuously walking the golf course.

We enjoy fond memories of those early days. Looking back, though, Ben likes to say that he knows I was somewhat messed up because I chose to date him; and in retrospect, he realizes his messy internal state. In the beginning, Ben liked that I didn't require much of him, and I liked being in charge. This relational dynamic significantly backfired on us a few years up the road.

I cleverly hid my heart in those days, too. I could chat with anyone about anything, but no one really knew me. I made sure that no one saw the real me. I didn't know the real me very well either, so how could they see her when I couldn't? This made it difficult for Ben and I to become genuinely close. Oh, we enjoyed hanging out together and all, but I never allowed him access to the deepest parts of my soul.

We were sexual early in our relationship. As we didn't know how to manage conflict, makeup sex served as a usual *fix* for any fight. We would bury the conflict beneath the sheets only to see it surface later in an explosive way. Our sexual sin eventually led to pregnancy during my final year of college. Ben shared years later that he was on the verge of ending our relationship when I told him.

I started work at the university hospital after graduation. We married soon after the birth of our daughter. Two years later, we had a son. With a job, two young children and a home to take care of, I became preoccupied with the responsibilities that came with those roles and grew gradually more distant from Ben.

Ben played golf in college after being a two-time state champion in high school. He played professionally but didn't have the skills to succeed at the top level. Without tournament golf, he lost the primary source of his identity. Then, undiagnosed depression enveloped him as he attempted an unsuccessful sales career. Unbeknownst to me, he pondered suicide. Fortunately, Ben called out to God before he attempted to kill himself. Three months later he quit drinking which had been a constant habit in his life since high school.

After he got sober, Ben lived a more reflective life. He explored the impact his drinking had on him as a man and a husband. He had always been a good dad when he was home but now realized the damage drinking in excess had on his soul and our relationship. His masculine soul emerged leading him in new directions as a man while I was still shallow and *in charge*.

To help with our financial situation he joined the Army Reserves and attended training on the East Coast for five months. Before he left, we took a walk on the dusty roads around my parents rural home. He asked, "Through all my drinking and everything, why did you stay with me?" I told him, "I always knew there was something good inside of you." This moment held a deeper connection than we were used to, a more honest conversation than we typically engaged in. Hope emerged in my soul.

And then we lived happily ever after. Not!

I moved us from Ben's hometown while he was at training as he anticipated a new career with a friend upon return. He felt he would never *grow up* if we didn't relocate. So, we began a new life in a new town, which was exciting but also somewhat dangerous. Meeting new people in this new place contributed to our downfall.

Our new locale wasn't all bad. We began to attend church there, and we became the *perfect* Christian couple and family. We were at church every time the doors were open, contributing to our already busy lifestyle. I realize now that I sought out church hoping for God to rescue me from the affair I felt brewing rather than hoping for a relationship with God that would rescue my soul.

With our newfound Christianity, Ben became considered the good guy at work rather than the party guy - a new role for him. Others admired him, and it felt good to be admired, especially when he didn't feel so admired at home by me due to my hidden and not-so-hidden criticism. He began going to lunch every workday with one of his female co-workers. His heart opened to her, and an emotional affair developed, but he always rationalized being a good Christian man by not having sex.

His attachment to her left me lonely and detached from him. That's when a salesman waltzed into my lab and pursued my lonely heart. I won't deny that it felt good being pursued, especially when I didn't feel so pursued at home by Ben. Church didn't do what I hoped for. It didn't rescue me from allowing myself to be caught in an affair. I jumped in and out of the affair for three years.

I was out of the affair when a job opened in medical sales. Unfortunately, my affair partner worked for the same company. Not knowing about my affair, Ben supported the idea of moving again and leaving his high stress job in the office of a large trucking company. He enrolled in seminary. Once again, we felt God guiding our paths, and He was, just not in the way we thought.

I thought I could handle traveling and training with my former affair partner, Bob. I was wrong. Ben and I agreed I would travel with Bob for a month. When the month ended, Bob and I continued to travel together. Ben became suspicious, and tensions grew between us over that summer.

I felt like a hypocrite and lower than scum. I knew what I was doing was wrong, so why still do it? I wanted to stop but couldn't. What does that say about me? I asked my affair partner, Bob, if his marriage also suffered because of our relationship. He replied, "Sex with my wife is great!" I felt used and deflated, so I decided to *finally* end the affair.

As August drew to an end, Ben figured out how to listen to my voicemail. He heard a message from Bob saying he would call the next day while Ben was at class. When Ben came home he asked if I had talked to Bob. I said no.

Ben confessed he listened to my voicemail. I felt like the breath was knocked from my lungs. I could barely squeak out the question, "What did you hear?" He told me. I realized I could hide no longer. I had to speak truth. That's when I heard, "You fuckin' whore!" The inquisition began. I answered question after question after question from Ben's broken and shattered heart. Once he could stand it no longer, he slammed the door, and I thought our relationship ended.

I curled up in a ball and sobbed. I wanted to kill myself, disappear or find Dr. Who to take me back in time to make different choices. But that wasn't going to happen. We had to journey back in time ourselves to uncover what led to our disastrous choices and heal them.

Come walk with us.

YOU DID WHAT!?

*B*etrayal slices the soul like an invisible knife thrust from nowhere. One moment life seems to be going along fine . . . thank you very much. The next moment, life is forever changed. Painfully changed. A thousand times the betrayed utters, "You did what!?" Through shock and numbness the betrayed seeks to make sense of his or her new reality.

Swings from bursts of rage to silently staring at the walls for hours become common following betrayal. Time is an ingredient in reconstructing one's heart. It takes time for the soul to catch up with what is true. The new reality is so different than what was previously believed.

Be kind to yourself as you adjust. Simple tasks may now seem challenging. Fits of anger can shoot out instantaneously. Know that your heart can be put back together, but it will never be the same. There is hope of a new reality that is good, yet first the pain must be faced.

STAY ALIVE

BEN

4 44 days. That's what the headline read the day U.S. hostages were released from Iran in January 1980. On the day of their release, they had been held hostage for 444 days. This is also the approximate number of days it took for Ann and I to really turn the corner and find release in dealing with our affairs.

Realize this process will take longer than you think. You may get to day 100 or 279 or 364 and wonder, "What's wrong with me? It's been so long; will we ever get past this? Why do I care? I wish I didn't care. I hate that I care. We've talked about it all again and again, so why won't it go away?"

Accept the process. Some days you'll make great strides forward and some days take two steps back. On those hard days it's important to stay engaged with the process, which includes staying engaged with each other. There are some days you will need to take a break and rest or play. Those days are an essential part of the process, too.

When hope wanes remember each day is a step through the darkness. So keep stepping. Do your best each day. Do your best on day 1 and 41 and 101 and 281 and 401. And somewhere out there - way beyond 90 days - you'll find freedom, and you'll know that you know that you know your marriage will make it, and you will be glad about it.

Especially early on, one or both of you may battle suicidal thoughts. If either of you need someone to talk to, the National Suicide Hotline number is 800-273-8255.

Ann battled suicidal thoughts as I did. I remember seeing her in the kitchen, her hair a thatchy nest, her t-shirt seemed two sizes too big on her fallen shoulders with her chin planted firmly into her collar. She pondered taking our Lab into the garage, turning the key and taking a road trip to nowhere.

At the same time, my pain was extremely intense. I'd wake up and feel great for a tenth of a second, but the pain would crash in again. Weary of the pain, I called our counselor.

He told me he could do nothing to take the pain away. He affirmed how hard this time in our lives must be. I forced the words through my mouth for the benefit of the one who had caused the pain. "Ann's thinking about killing herself."

He had me put her on the phone. The theme of his message resembled the message from *The Last of the Mohicans* in the waterfall scene. "Stay alive. Call me if you think you'll do something. Stay alive. Call me if you are going to kill yourself. Stay alive."

The words from Hawkeye to Cora echo God's words to us. "Stay alive, I will find you. Survive. Stay alive, no matter what occurs. I will find you. No matter how long it takes, no matter how far."

Ann did stay alive, and God did rescue and heal and reveal himself to Ann. And now, through her, He reveals and shares his story of love and redemption.

It's hard to get through this crap, especially the first 30 days, but know that you have no idea of God's plans for you.

Stay alive, no matter what occurs. He will find you.

What wild thoughts is your pain producing? If you are suicidal, call your counselor or the 800 number above.

PRESSURE AND TIME

BEN

*A*re you willing to stay in the prison of a marriage with little or no intimacy; or are you willing to pay the price of redemption - even if it is costly?

Consider Andy Dufresne in *Shawshank Redemption*. Andy lived in prison for nearly 20 years for murders he didn't commit. He lived in a situation that would seemingly never end. That's how dealing with an affair felt to me. I wasn't sure how I would ever get through the crap to live happily with Ann again.

In the movie, Andy used a small geologist's hammer to tunnel out of the limestone prison. His friend, Red, said, "I remember thinking it would take a man 600 years to tunnel out of the wall with it. Andy did it in less than 20." Red continued, "Andy loved geology . . . Geology is the study of pressure and time. That's all it takes really. Pressure and time."

Like Andy, we have a choice. We can play it safe and go back to our prison cell, or we can risk crawling through a pipe filled with crap that goes on longer than we ever imagined. We can endure to emerge in freedom. Pressure and time are part of affair recovery.

Keep going. Be willing to keep going, even if it hurts so bad you want to stop, even if the crap stinks so bad you want to vomit. When almost every ounce in you wants to turn around, keep going. As long as you keep moving - if both spouses are moving, even if at different paces - there is hope.

Don't give up.

We've seen this process of redemption in our lives. When other couples seek our guidance, trapped in pain following an affair, we help them experience the rescue and deliverance to freedom that filled our souls.

You really can do this even if you don't see the way out of the prison cell right now. Know that God sees you. He sees ahead beyond the pain that obstructs your vision of the future.

For us, the journey through all the crap to find freedom in our relationship with God and in our marriage proved worthwhile. At times all we can do is raise our hands in worship to the mystery of a God who redeems the mess of our greatest wounds and our greatest sins.

What fears do you have about committing to this recovery process with your spouse?

THE DANCING WORK OF PAIN

ANN

I didn't grow up in a family that shared feelings, so I never really learned how. I often answered the question "how do you feel?" with "I don't know" and truly meant it. I didn't know my inner world. After I revealed my affair, I didn't want to deal with the hurt and pain that began slicing up my inner world. I felt like a failure with a capital F. I thought it would be easier if I ended it all right then and there. Yeah, right. Easier for who? We had no gun, knives are too messy, and the strongest medication in the cabinet was Tylenol. So I chose, we chose, to live in the chaos that followed the revelation.

In choosing to live in the chaos, my hurt and pain looked me square in the eye and challenged me to a staring contest. I dared not look away even though I didn't like it. Facing my pain brought up mounds of shame and guilt. I wanted to run! But gradually I learned the value of sitting with my pain.

An author named Lauren Slater wrote *Welcome to My Country: A Therapist's Memoir of Madness*. Slater suffered from abuse and self-harm as a child and evolved into a therapist. She offers these words on pain and suffering:

"And so I began, slowly...to think about staying in suffering instead of always trying to climb out of it. Do not mistake me. I don't mean I learned to embrace pain, whose boiling body frightens me as it scalds the skin of its victims, nor, in the parlance of New Age-speak, to accept pain, for acceptance is far too sweet a word, and I doubt very many people loosen their limbs and lie pliantly in the lap of hurting. I mean I learned, quite simply--in these technical times, when the hope for new remedies is daily dangled before our eyes--to acknowledge pain, to sit still in its mysterious presence and feel helpless... What sets me apart (from my most troubled clients) is simply a learned ability to manage the blades of deep pain with a little bit of dexterity. Mental health doesn't mean making the pains go away. I don't believe they ever go away...*I have not healed so much as learned to sit still and wait while pain does it dancing work, trying not to panic or twist in ways that make the blades tear deeper, finally infecting the wounds.*"

There really is no way around the pain from an affair. If you thrash around or go berserk while the blades are nearby you'll be cut deeper and bleed more. If you turn to drugs, alcohol, porn or sex to medicate the pain, again you thrash and cause more pain. The only way to deal with the pain from an affair is to move straight through it, slowly.

Ben and I moved straight through the pain of the affair the best we could. How we handle pain and suffering has a direct correlation to the depth of our relationships. The more we run from our pain, the more we run from intimacy. The more we stay engaged with our pain and reality, the deeper our relationships.

Face the truth, and let it do its dancing work on your soul.

How have you avoided pain and suffering?

EXHAUSTION
IS ENEMY NUMBER ONE

BEN

"The number one enemy of Christian spiritual formation today is exhaustion. We are made to spend a large portion of our existence essentially doing nothing (sleep). The failure to do so results in damage to physical health, loss of energy and decreased productivity. And our sleep depravation hurts others."

~JAMES BRYAN SMITH IN 'GOOD AND BEAUTIFUL GOD'

The purpose of the Sabbath is to stop and take stock of your soul. Generally speaking, we won't be able to do that unless we practice the discipline of sleep.

In these initial weeks of dealing with an affair restful or adequate sleep is lacking. Pain and chaos make it difficult to truly enter a restful sleep. Many conversations between Ann and I took place deep into the morning hours. We gave each other permission to wake the other up and talk any time day or night if something felt like it just couldn't wait. We built closeness during those bleary-eyed conversations.

Affairs are sometimes precipitated by ignored busyness and soul exhaustion. A smooth talker comes along who brings (what appears to be) life into that depleted heart; the spark ignites under the illusion until the inevitable explosion sprays fragments of pain in all directions.

Ann's soul bowed under the weight of exhaustion when her affair started. She drove our youngest to daycare, worked eight hours, picked the kids up after work, fed them dinner and shuttled each to activities, helped lead some of those activities then collapsed at night. Repeat. Repeat.

I drove to work before six and arrived home after six. Additionally, I volunteered extra hours on weekends to help us climb out of debt, and I soldiered up for my Army Reserve drill one weekend a month.

Our soul-numbing schedule should have stood out like icy roads during a heat wave. We didn't notice. We believed we were being good parents since our kids participated in basketball, Scouts, music and plays concurrently.

Post affair we limited the kids to one activity at a time. And you know what? They liked it. Ann and Stephanie rolled into the parking lot for music lessons early and our daughter looked at Ann and said, "Wow! We're on time." Our busyness stressed our kids too, but we were oblivious to it.

Ann left her full-time job during the week and took a job working weekend nights following the affair. Essentially, she got to be a stay-at-home mom during the week. This allowed her time to *do nothing*. This allowed her time to rest, time for her soul to catch up. Rest was a key ingredient in healing her soul.

Ann says of this time, "I was able to finally openly grieve with Ben instead of in a corner by myself, hiding. Most of all, I could begin to rest. I no longer had to be a hard-charging, frenetic woman because Ben had become the protector of our family. I could rest. In that rest is where I truly began to know I was a beloved daughter of the King. I began to become the woman that God designed me to be instead of the woman the world demanded that I be."

Smith offers soul-training exercises in his book and the first exercise is sleep. Follow his suggestion (and ours) and be intentional about getting plenty of sleep during this chaotic time. This week, sleep until you can't sleep anymore. Stay in bed until you are fully rested. Let your family know what you are doing. Also, try to get at least seven hours on three different days. More days would be better, but you have to start somewhere.

Slow down, let your soul catch up with you.

Where are you experiencing busyness and exhaustion in your life?

BETRAYAL
AND ROBERT THE BRUCE

BEN

My heart exploded the moment I learned about Ann's affair. I felt like pieces were in Orlando, San Diego, Portland, Oregon and Portland, Maine. I felt a surge of rage where my heart once rested. Fortunately, my heart didn't fully shatter. It felt like a jigsaw puzzle flipped haphazardly out of the box, but it was not destroyed.

Surely no one *really* understood how I felt. I wasn't very good at telling anyone about the depth of angst and pain trolling my soul. Who could I trust with this mess inside? I talked to my pastor whose first wife had left him.

He said, "Don't you wish you'd never found out?" I didn't even have to think about my answer. No. It hurt like hell, but if our marriage was to have any chance we had to deal with the truth of our actions.

Gratefully, my chaplain in the reserves recommended a counselor. What on earth would the counselor want to do with my shell-shocked self?

After we told him the basics of our story he looked at me with kindness and said, "You're in a lot of pain, aren't you?"

Relief poured in. This man saw me. He saw the puzzle pieces and saw the picture of my pained soul. Though I struggled with trusting anyone at this point, I gave him my trust as best I could.

Another person who understood me was Mel Gibson.

I am deeply impacted by a scene from *Braveheart* involving betrayal. William Wallace, played by Mel Gibson, goes into the Battle of Falkirk believing the nobles are aligned with his band of commoners. Earlier, at a contentious meeting, Robert the Bruce, the future king of Scotland, convinced Wallace to join forces with the nobles. The Bruce chased after Wallace, offered his hand and said, "Unite us!"

Wallace clasped his hand and believed they would soon conquer the English and earn Scotland's independence. At a key point in the battle, Wallace signals for the nobles to charge in on horseback. They slink away with their 30 pieces of silver, land and titles. King Longshanks of England bought them out.

Wallace takes a real and symbolic arrow almost straight to the heart. Like a wild-eyed and wounded animal, he grabs a horse and rides after Longshanks who long ago murdered Wallace's father and many in his village. As Wallace approaches Longshanks, an English horseman is told to protect the king.

The horseman, face hidden by armored headgear, rides at the charging Wallace tripping Wallace's horse with his lance. The horseman dismounts and moves close to Wallace who plays dead. Wallace grabs him, knife poised to slit his throat, rips off the headgear of the screaming Englishman and discovers not an Englishman but Robert the Bruce. Betrayed! I remember losing my breath as I watched.

As an actor, Mel Gibson nails betrayal. He embodies shock and how in a moment a central foundation of one's world is instantaneously blown up. That actually doesn't even come close to describing it. With other English approaching, Wallace lays down in the field, not caring if he lives or dies. The first time I saw this scene I instantly felt understood. They got me. After the rage subsided, I just wanted to lay down. I didn't really care what happened to me.

Exposed, the Bruce comes to his senses. He sees other English soldiers approaching, and screams at Wallace to "Get up!" The Irishman rides in just in time, and with the Bruce's help gets Wallace on a horse and gallops to safety.

Later, the scene shifts back to the dark and foggy battlefield. Wide-eyed, shocked and stunned, the Bruce stumbles through the brutally and fatally wounded bodies of his fellow countrymen. After surveying the slaughter, he realizes their demise came from his betrayal. He falls to his knees, haunted by the carnage he created.

Ann connects with the Bruce's walk through the dead and wounded, his eyes glazed over. Like Bruce, she never imagined the pain her betrayal would cause me, our kids, herself and other relationships in her life. She never imagined the carnage her affair created. Fortunately for both of us, her eyes were now fully opened and focused on becoming a changed woman.

Where do you connect with the emotions of betrayal as Betrayed or Betrayer as portrayed by William Wallace and Robert the Bruce?

BETRAYAL, WORSHIP
AND MT. RUSHMORE

BEN

Three weeks after I learned of the affair, I stormed into the house, cussed at my wife, threw my book bag against the kitchen wall, packed a bag and like any barely sane, wracked-with-pain cuckold would do, I set out on a drive to Mt. Rushmore. I had been reading a book on the letters of Thomas Jefferson, you see.

So, I drove. I traveled 500 miles the first day and found a room. I drove into Rapid City before noon the next morning.

I decided to take a horse ride, part of some tour of Black Hills lore. My guide's name was Jack. Jack and I didn't get very far before he asked what brought me there. I told him all about it. He hesitated a moment, and then began to talk. He was a former pastor from Rhode Island. His wife left him for another man, divorced Jack, and the church board asked Jack to resign. I don't know what the odds were of running into a man like Jack, but the *Twilight Zone* theme song played in my head throughout our ride.

God brought two hurting brothers together to help us find understanding and compassion in the midst of our stinging ache. We talked non-stop for an hour. It brings a smile to my face to remember Jack saying near the end of our ride, "I guess I ought to tell you about one thing that I am supposed to. That barn over there..."

After the horse ride I stood on a rock - a big rock that I found after driving over the pigtail bridges. As I stood on the rock with pain throbbing through my chest, all through me really, something prompted me to look up. I saw the glory of God's creation in the waves of rolling hills with green, brilliant green, pine trees. The beauty captured me.

I took a breath and said, "God, I hurt so much." I took another breath and said, "God, this is so beautiful." "I hurt so much. This is so beautiful." And on I went writhing alternately with joy and pain. I took all of who I was at that moment and went to God. Pure worship. I didn't think of what was right or acceptable. I just was, and was with God.

Throughout the affair recovery process I wondered if God was there. If He was there I wondered if He knew what He was doing. Along the way He helped me with glimpses of His heart like my time with Jack and my worship on the rock. These experiences helped me learn to detest the saying 'Check your world at the door' when I go to church. If you do that then it's pretty easy to check your Lord at the door on your way out. God wants all of us. He wants our junk, our pettiness, our anger, our hurt, our laughs, our smiles and our radiance. He wants to bring it all into His presence and transform darkness into His Light.

So, I ached. I beamed. He transformed and is transforming and will continue to transform all my mess and all my glory so He and I may be closer and so His kingdom may shine even brighter.

Taking our deepest pain to God is a form of worship. How have you experienced this?

WHY BETRAYAL HURTS
SO MUCH

BEN

For some time, I suspected Ann may be having an affair. But somewhere deep inside I instinctively knew how much pain that would bring. So we developed a dance: I would question, she would lie, I'd say okay, and we'd move on. "Second verse same as the first!" When Ann disclosed her affair, I faced the most painful truth I hope I'll ever encounter. I also had to look in the mirror at my own failures.

Betrayal is acting in a way contrary to the *assumed expectations* in the relationship. Of the expectations we bring into marriage, telling the truth ranks pretty high. On their wedding day a husband and wife become bound together, joined on the same side; and it is assumed it will stay that way.

Ann didn't expect me to become emotionally closer to another woman. Yet, I chose to do that. If something good happened I looked forward to telling the other woman at work rather than Ann. I didn't overtly lie to Ann about my emotional entanglement, but I sure did lie through omission.

I assumed Ann would never actually have sex with someone else since I didn't. I'm glad I didn't have sex with another woman and also glad my expectation was that she wouldn't. It just made it hurt like hell when I finally found out the truth.

When the affair came out our Christian walk seemed solid. We were overconfident in many ways and immature, too. The affair did begin before Ann regained a solid footing in her faith. I say that to highlight that a couple shares assumed moral values. The more we moved towards God, the more our morals were in line. Affairs serve as Exhibit A: we don't always live out our stated morals.

An assumption of enduring love in marriage remains a constant. Even if events and a lack of attention erode the relationship there still exists the belief that we are married, we married out of love so we'll get to the good times again. Yet, expressing love looks different to each person. And expressing love in a way that misses the heart of your spouse precipitates the erosion of that love.

So, the quality of the *perceived connection* typically determines the level of betrayal. Even if the marriage isn't going particularly well, the perceived connection usually runs pretty deep based on the amount of time spent dating, the wedding day, shared dreams, shared story, shared home, etc. All that sharing, even if the relationship grows distant, leads to a *sense* of connection even in the absence of a *real* connection. It is possible to live in denial in our marriages for quite some time. Reality covered up by denial spews its toxic self all over when an affair gets revealed.

The denial of both betrayed and betrayer explodes on the day of the revelation of the affair because both have lost their idols. Idols, in this sense, refer to finding life in something other than God. The betrayed loses the idol of their perception of who they thought their spouse was. I didn't really believe Ann was capable of an affair much less capable of concealing it for years. I held her up as the woman who was supposed to make me feel good about who I am as a man. That's exactly what men do with pornography. Ouch! We are all married to a spouse who is incredibly glorious and also capable of heinous sin. I lost the idol that my wife was all glory and her purpose was to make me feel good. I mean, I knew she sinned but I didn't think she was capable of *that*.

The betrayer loses the idol that precipitated the betrayal - the affair partner, pornography, drugs, etc. All of a sudden, their idol stops making the world wonderful. Their idol causes problems instead of soothing their soul. Also, his or her portrayed image shatters like a china teacup thrown on a tile floor. The wonderful person projected looks different now exposed in lies and deception. Just ask anyone whose name appeared on the recent Ashley Madison hack.

Both spouses lose the image of the ideal marriage. The truth that the marriage isn't perfect - or anywhere near perfect - stuns both spouses. Most people will say their marriage is okay regardless of the actual state of the relationship. Everything looked great for us on the outside. We were moving towards dreams of seminary, good paying jobs and buying a brand new home. I was seduced by it, too. When the truth of the affair came out, it all meant squat. It was all rubbish compared to a real relationship with God and a close, transparent and monogamous marriage.

Our marriage was exposed as lacking - lacking far more than I knew it was. We weren't the couple on the go, on the rise. We were all of a sudden the couple in chaos. It was a huge battering ram to the soul for both of us.

From a broader view, what idols are being shattered in your marriage as you enter the recovery process?

SHATTERED HEART

BEN

*I*ntense emotions surface when a betrayal is discovered. Trust shatters. Hearts shatter. The illusion of walking lockstep down the path of life explodes leaving a gaping, gnarly crater. The couple careens into the bottom, bloody, stunned and disoriented.

For the betrayed, there is traumatic aftershock. Imagine you're at the movie theater, and the digital surround sound kicks in and you feel a sudden bam! The theater shakes, and noise reverberates. Similarly, betrayal impacts your soul to the core.

My first response was to yell and scream and cuss and go all B-movie on Ann. I stomped about interrogating her for details of their relationship. I threw howcouldyou comments at her repeatedly. Hours later, I'd feel worn down and need a break. The immensity of the lies and deception seemingly grew to be measured in tons.

I became irritable and aggressive. Every slight, or perceived slight, was magnified a thousand times precipitating an angry spewing of venom. I don't know what's more fragile than egg shells, but that's what Ann walked on. Unpredictability became the indicator of my anger.

When I wasn't aggressive, I was stunned. I looked at my life and wondered who it belonged to. The denial was broken, but my soul took a while to absorb *all* the truth. I experienced the drastic morphing of my life and couldn't keep up with it. It's hard to put into words. I was aware and involved but felt distant and also incredibly numb.

I could sit in our over-sized recliner for the duration of the day, staring at nothing in particular. The reverberation from the revelation still trembled in my soul. I sat still, letting the pain work on me. I didn't need a TV. Mental tapes of haunting visions kept me company.

I guess you could say I was struck dumb by the enormity of the betrayal. I wasn't belted in the chair, but I couldn't seem to move other than to rock an inch or two when my soul twitched. I spent hours a day listening to my own breath.

I sat obsessing about Ann's affair. The images and unanswered questions rolled around my brain like wet clothes in the dryer. I wanted more answers and details. My illusion was that more details would lead to more understanding. If I could understand it, make sense of it rationally, then I wouldn't ache so intensely. So, I interrogated Ann.

"What about the time here, and what happened when you went there? How come you did this? Why didn't you do that? Did you ever think what you were risking? Why didn't you tell me? Did you meet there? Did he ever come here? Did his wife know???? Tell me it all again."

I believed that knowing more would ease the pain. And it worked . . . for a millisecond. The pain would pour back through viaducts and then, whataboutthis and whatwasthedealonthat swelled over and over and over again.

Along with the pain I felt rabid hatred for my wife. I hurt, and I hated the one who made me hurt.

Yet, that wasn't all I felt. Ann and I had been through so much already. She was the bride of my youth. I loved her. I felt crazy, as the pain was screaming to seek comfort in Ann's arms and then realizing the one who betrayed me was the one holding me. It felt good; and I hated it.

Write a few words about your love for your spouse? And write a few words about your anger at your spouse?

THE BETRAYER HAS A SOUL

ANN

*W*ho cares about the emotional upheaval the betrayer experiences? I caused destruction and heartache to my husband and family. Why should anyone care about the impact on my soul?

We should care because the betrayer has a soul. He/she has a wounded soul, not just from the impact of the betrayal, but most likely from deep wounding carefully and not-so-expertly hidden for years. Opening the floodgates of hell on my soul prompted an in-depth exploration of the recesses of my dark and lonely heart. I wanted to know how I was able to make the choices that put my family at risk?

The initial trauma of the revelation of the affair carries significant weight. It is tied to the disbelief that we could actually be *that* person, that we could make *those* choices. People who know me only post-healing from the affair say, 'That wasn't really you, right?' Well, my healing journey revealed that it really was me.

During the affair the dark expanses of my soul grew and covered the light, dimming it to the point I wasn't even sure the light shone any more. Not really anyway. An artificial light was there, kind of like fluorescent bulbs in an office. They flicker and become annoying and hurt your eyes if you're exposed to them too long cause they're not real, they're artificial, just like me. The real light – like sunshine on a beautiful, clear Colorado morning – that light wasn't there anymore either. And the trauma of the revelation not only broke all the fluorescent bulbs, it all but extinguished the real life-giving light.

Not even having the artificial light to sustain me, I began to feel incredibly numb. I didn't have the light to enable me to feel even false feelings. I also didn't want to feel any feelings. I didn't want to feel the pain I caused Ben. I didn't want to feel the pain I caused my beautiful children. I didn't want to feel the pain I began to feel as I peeled back the layers covering my wounds and shame. Some days, I lurched around like a zombie with no real purpose. Routine tasks became difficult because all I wanted to do was *play dead* because that's how I felt. Dead. I wished I were dead.

This desire for death was compounded by my frustration with Ben's constant demand for details. We would go through Twenty Questions, round one. He appeared somewhat satisfied with my answers, and just as I began to breathe again he'd start another round. Combined with his need (and it really is a need in the beginning of healing and rebuilding trust) to know my whereabouts and activities every second of every day, I felt trapped some days. Zero freedom. Zero life. Death looked quite appealing.

Realizing that my worldly sorrow felt like death began to create a shift in me. Worldly sorrow is sorrow about being found out. In 2 Corinthians 7:10 it says: "Distress that drives us to God does that. It turns us around. It gets us back in the way of salvation. We never regret that kind of pain. But those who let distress drive them away from God are full of regrets, end up on a deathbed of regrets." I ended up on my deathbed from the trauma, numbness and frustration rather than allowing the experience of my pain to drive me to God.

Once I began to allow myself to experience the impact of my sin and the ensuing pain, ALL of it - even going back to my early years, I began to experience what Paul goes on to describe as the overflow of Godly sorrow: "And now, isn't it wonderful all the ways in which this distress has goaded you closer to God?

You're more alive, more concerned, more sensitive, more reverent, more human, more passionate, more responsible. Looked at from any angle, you've come out of this with purity of heart" (2 Corinthians 7:11). (emphasis mine) Wow! That's what I really wanted. That's what my soul longed for. I just never knew it. I just went about finding it in ALL the wrong ways, especially in my affair.

Once I could *truly* begin to grieve the carnage created by my actions, once I could *truly* begin to grieve the pain I caused my husband, once I could *truly* begin to grieve the pain I caused my children, once I could truly begin to grieve the pain buried deep in my soul, then I could begin to *truly* believe the radiant light that God placed in my soul was *truly* there. For God to see. For others to see. For me to see.

As the betrayer, where do you find yourself in the above passage from 2 Corinthians?

As the betrayed, what are your immediate needs from your spouse?

HOW LONG O LORD?

American culture trends toward the bright, pretty and fun not the dark, messy and sad. Grief and sorrow aren't topics we naturally gravitate toward. Most people don't want to talk about suffering much less intentionally experience it. Yet, affairs bring suffering, and eventually the losses that brought the suffering must be named and acknowledged.

One challenge with openly suffering is the response it brings from well-meaning friends. These friends are often uncomfortable with suffering and sorrow. They don't know what to say and may be afraid to *catch* your suffering like a communicable disease. Unfortunately, these friends will try to explain your suffering, avoid you or fix your suffering. Author and former pastor Eugene Peterson says, "Suffering attracts fixers the way roadkill attracts vultures."

Explanations and glib advice don't cure your suffering and sorrow. Find friends to assist with engaging the truth, pay attention to your heart and express your emotions. This is the path through grief. The path winds up and down, round and round through scary territory. Fear, pain, anger and sadness accompany you for this trek. You may wonder if you're really getting anywhere and query the sky, "How long O Lord?" I don't know the specific answer, but I can tell you one answer. You'll grieve longer than you want. But keep going. Eventually, the path of grief ushers you to green, love-filled pastures.

GO EAST, YOUNG MAN

BEN AND ANN

Grieving isn't just about the death of someone you love. We suffer *deaths* of various flavors throughout our lives. Life isn't exactly like a box of chocolates, Forest Gump. It's more like Bertie Bott's Every Flavour Beans, Harry Potter. Sometimes we get great tastes like banana and bacon; other times we gag on rotten eggs or petrol.

My friend, Krista, understands the sour flavors you are experiencing now, "Every day we experience death. The death of dreams, misconceptions, illusions. The death of vibrancy and enthusiasm. The death of hope. The death of courage. The death of confidence. The death of faith. The death of trust. More often than any of us ever expect, life stuns us with the sudden wrenching away of a loved one, a devastating diagnosis, or a conversation that begins with the chilling words, 'There's something I've got to tell you.'"

In our stunned state, we make daily choices whether to numb our souls or to face the pain. To grow, we must allow ourselves to grieve our woundedness, which stems from ways we have been hurt and ways we have hurt others that lead to the loss of relationship and intimacy. The maze of grief through these wounds eventually leads to extraordinary encounters with God.

We had much to grieve following the revelation of the affair. One of the best decisions we made involved facing the pain each day. Even though a constant wash of pain poured over us, we figured there was still only so much pain to navigate. If we managed to make it through the pain, we didn't want mistrust constantly snaking around our relationship two decades hence. So we walked with grief through the pain.

Grief takes many forms. Practical ways to grieve include: walking, staring at the walls, writing, painting, dancing, working out and playing sports, beating the bed with a whiffle ball bat, praying the Psalms, simply telling God you hurt, talking with a good friend, spending unhurried time with a friend where conversation is light and/or deep, laughing at the absurdity of the situation and praying with Jesus at the crucifixion. Perhaps you have a couple other ways in mind.

However you grieve, heed these words from Gerald Sittser, who lost his mom, wife and one of his daughters in the same car wreck. He shares in *A Grace Disguised*: "The quickest way to reach the sun and light of day is not to run west, chasing the setting sun, but to head east, plunging into the darkness until one comes to the sunrise."

So, go east, young man and young woman. We grieve any loss in our lives, not just death. Our response to loss determines whether we can give and receive love again or become tight-souled and bitter.

What wounds are you aware of today? Be as specific as possible.

REFUSAL TO GRIEVE

BEN

$\mathfrak{M}$any problems result from a refusal to grieve. In affair recovery, there is much to grieve. Loss of trust, dreams, respect . . . most of what felt solid and sure.

Yet, we refuse to grieve, because it freakin' hurts!

Ultimately, facing the pain and sadness as squarely as one can is the quickest way through it.

In his book, *The Return of the Prodigal Son*, Henri Nouwen explores the world from the view of the wayward son, the self-righteous older brother and the grace-giving father from Luke 11:15-32. He asks the reader to take an introspective look and honestly expose how he/she is like each character in the story. In the book, Nouwen offers this definition of grief: "Grief is the discipline of the heart that sees the sin of the world and knows itself to be the sorrowful price of freedom without which love cannot bloom."

Let's go backwards through this quote. Without grief, love cannot bloom. If we refuse to grieve, there are places in one's soul that cannot experience giving or receiving love. The wound becomes hard like a diamond, trapping the blood and tenderness inside. With grief, love can flourish. In other words, experiencing sadness and pain paves the pathway that expands our capacity for love.

Grief is the sorrowful price of freedom. Our sorrow costs us. Dearly it costs us. That sorrowful price allows us to escape a prison. However, those who refuse to grieve remain trapped in the wounds of the past. This causes these unprocessed wounds to remain fresh chaining us to the past. At some point, we all have to own our stories and the pain and joy that come with them. The worst statement one can utter in affair recovery is "we must never talk about this affair again."

If our sorrow frees us, our avoidance and denial lock us up in solitary confinement.

Grief sees the sin of the world with eyes wide open. This includes our own self-centeredness and the self-centeredness of others. Sin causes pain. Grief moves toward that pain and says, "Tell me more about it." It takes heroic courage to grieve this way.

Grief is a discipline of the heart. It does take courage to walk into it. It's easier in the short run to bury our souls in alcohol, drugs, busyness at church, the internet, porn, football on TV, our kids, etc. To face it every day, as much as one can, takes discipline and choice when there are 15 trillion ways to numb our souls.

Have courage. Face the truth. Feel the hurt, the anger, the sadness, the rage, the nothing; and eventually - though I can't tell you how long eventually is - at some point, as you pay the sorrowful price of freedom, your wounds will become the soil of verdant growth.

What frightens you about entering the grieving process?

TOMB TIME

BEN

The previous two Easters we've gathered with friends to read the Book of John aloud. Our black chair with multicolored circles serves as the designated reading chair. We alternate reading a chapter at a time aloud. John wrote 21 chapters so we take a brief break after chapters 7 and 14. Altogether we experience three hours of stunning oration. The oration isn't stunning because James Earl Jones or Meryl Streep has joined us. It's stunning because our little group, our common community of everyday voices, speak the profound story of mercy, suffering and life of God.

Hearing the word read in a plethora of voices impacts my soul. To hear the Gospel in both feminine and masculine voice reaches new and uncharted waters inside me. Also, readers remark how their chapter (rather Jesus through the chapter) tenderly touches his or her soul.

I am impacted by Jesus' own tender dealings with those deemed *less than* throughout the reading. He heals the lame and blind, reveals his true self to an outcast woman at a well, protects and speaks words of life to a woman caught in adultery, and provides meaning for his friends with regards to his life on earth and his death on the cross.

Ultimately, the cross gets me. As the evening progresses, a slow-motion dread builds within, hearing the dogged, inexorable march of Jesus to his crucifixion on the cross. I grow fond of Jesus as his narrative, the narrative of God on earth, rests on our room and my heart. I don't want him, so loving and courageous, to die.

But die he does. His death tears at my scalp and back, vibrates in my wrists and shins, and pounds my chest, where my grief tends to physically reside. Even though I know the story isn't over, I ache and ache and wish there was another way the story could go than persistently and unavoidably through the dead center of the cross.

The Book of John records the burial of Jesus but doesn't say much about his followers during that terrible 36 hours or so while he is in the tomb. Tomb time - that's what I call most of affair recovery. The great trauma has happened, and the resurrection isn't yet known to be true. It's a mysterious, painful time.

After John and Peter take note of the absence of Jesus' body in the tomb, they leave, yet Mary Magdalene remains at the tomb weeping. She weeps just as Jesus wept over the death of Lazarus. Staying in her grief leads her to an encounter with Jesus. I believe his approaching a woman - a woman in tears - holds meaning.

Always the question asker, He asks, "Why do you weep? Whom do you seek?" It almost seems playful. He then speaks her name, "Mary," and she recognizes him. He is risen!

Grief provides a pathway from our story to the larger story of God. His life and interaction with others touches our deepest longings to be seen and loved. His death rips at our hearts touching the part that was ripped by the revelation of an affair.

In tomb time, we reside in mystery. The ache becomes a real part of our lives and we get somewhat used to it, though we are most always ready for it to leave.

With his resurrection and the speaking of our names we know God sees us in our grief. He comes toward us with good intentions for our hearts, even though he allowed great pain. He comes in peace.

Reflect for yourself on the same questions Jesus asks Mary: Why do you weep? Whom (and what) do you seek?

PERMISSION TO GRIEVE

BEN AND ANN

Following an affair there is much to grieve. But isn't grief about a death? Certainly, death brings loss and grieving, but grieving and loss aren't limited to the death of a friend or loved one. We grieve more than just death.

Angela Thomas in her great book on the feminine soul, *Do You Think I'm Beautiful,* said, "What if living means that suffering cannot be avoided?"

That's a foreign concept to a culture that believes we can figure out a way to do life that leads to an upward spiral. The illusion projects that life can always get better and better if we do it right. And, of course, we can figure out how to do it right. Right? Wrong!

Life, more roller coaster than upward spiral, has ascents and descents. Dealing with an affair - obvious descent. Perhaps you are wondering if it is okay to grieve. Can we give you something that many individuals need with regards to those downward plummets in life?

We give you permission to grieve your losses.

What losses? Here are a few possibilities. Was there job loss? Did you have to move? Do you have to see the affair partner often or occasionally due to living in a small town or same place of employment? Was there a pregnancy from the affair? How about the loss of trust in the marriage? Did you lose a sense of specialness because there was sex outside of marriage?

That should get you started. Those are significant losses, and it is healthy to grieve those losses or whatever losses exist in your situation. We wish it wasn't so, but we are fallen people in a fallen world. Sin brings pain. Pain brings loss. Loss leads to grieving. And God is okay with it because God grieves.

Consider the story of Saul. God chose Saul to be king. He disobeyed God in a battle and after that battle by not killing everyone and keeping some livestock. God removes his blessing on Saul, and Scripture tells us, "...God was sorry he ever made Saul king in the first place."

God felt sorrow. God grieved. Some folks think that God knows how every little detail will turn out. This may sound heretical to some, but we don't think so given this text. He is omniscient, but it certainly doesn't appear like He saw this one coming. That brought loss to God.

Suffering and sorrow are a part of life. They can't be avoided. *A Grace Disguised* by Gerald Sittser is a powerful read regardless of the reason for your loss. He says this about Jesus and suffering: "God embraced human experience and lived with all the ambiguities and struggles that characterize life on earth. In the end he became a victim of injustice and hatred, suffered horribly on the cross, and died an ignominious death. The sovereign God came in Jesus to suffer with us and to suffer for us . . . His sovereignty did not protect him from loss." Jesus suffered loss.

God knows that we'll suffer, and the astounding truth that He will suffer with us blows us away. Give yourself permission to grieve your losses and be blown away by meeting God most intimately in the depths of your suffering and sorrow.

What losses are you experiencing? How did your family handle grieving in your childhood?

SO LONG TO ILLUSIONS

BEN AND ANN

Grief strips away the pretense of life. Grief is about being honest with life and feeling the pain it brings.

First, I {Ben} had to accept the pain after the revelation of the affair. There was the initial shock and trauma with the why, why, why and how could yous. Slowly, I began to realize that this was indeed my life. The pain crashed in a split second after I opened my eyes each morning.

I grieved losing the ideal Ann. In my mind, I believed Ann could be tempted, but when it came to actually shaking her jeans down to the ground with another guy, I pictured her saying no before that point. Eventually, I had to learn that she was and is capable of making such a mistake; I had to own that I was, too.

I was lulled into this sense somewhat by a conversation I had with a woman I was emotionally enmeshed with. I brought up the topic of sex with her. She said, "Ben, you don't want to do that. I did that, and it ruined my marriage. You have two young kids and a chance at a good marriage." A counselor helped me see that if she had been more willing, as Ann's partner was, that most likely we would have ended up flinging our jeans to the ground, too.

The other side of this paradigm was learning to love the real Ann. Ann was capable of having an affair. I owned that she could sin with the best of them. I also owned and grieved the ways I failed to love her well. I left her lonely by my emotional affair, left her unchosen, left her with most of the burden of toting around and caring for our kids. I lost focus of all the wonder and glory that resides in her beautiful, feminine soul. None of that excuses the affair, but it makes her vulnerability to an affair understandable, and it was important to grieve my part in our shiny-on-the-outside and gnarly-on-the-inside marriage.

In my grief, I didn't care to B.S. about life. Pretenses were dropped. In a scene in the movie *American Beauty*, Kevin Spacey reaches that place. At the urging of his wife, he tells his daughter about his day at work. "Janie, today I quit my job. And then I told my boss to go fuck himself, and then I blackmailed him for almost $60,000. . . pass the asparagus." After some arguing with his wife, he ends up tossing the plate of asparagus through the window.

While I'm not advocating that, I'm giving you a peak into my soul at the time. During an argument near the kitchen table with Ann I slammed a chair into the linoleum. (Again, I'm not saying that was the best thing to do.) A spindle broke. Ann pointed and said, "That's grandma's chair." I said, "Fuck Grandma's chair! How about my broken soul!?"

I didn't want to pretend anymore. Following an earlier moment in time where I called out to God to take me back or show me the way, I felt free and had a growing healthy sense of self. But as we increased our church attendance I gradually put my masks back on, though this time instead of the *party guy* I wore the *good guy* mask. Post affair I was sick of masks, didn't know which way was up, but I was going to feel what I felt. Grief is messy because anger is a huge part of it.

I {Ann} didn't feel I had the right to grieve. I was the one who created the mess we were living. I didn't feel worthy to release the soul-healing balm of tears that could wash away my pain.

I felt a deep sense of guilt and shame for the choice I made. I always believed that if Ben were to have an affair that would be the straw that broke the camel's back so to speak. I would feel justified divorcing him. And then, what did I do? I did the exact thing I thought would be cause for divorce. Initially, my tears were more about the sorrow over the choices I made rather than for the pain I caused.

And I caused Ben much pain. Given our history of not addressing conflict, I never imagined he would be so hurt and show it in such volatile ways. I thought it would be one more thing that would create some silence for a few days and then we'd sweep it under the rug along with so many years of trash. As we began to shake out the rug and see what was really under there, as we began to remove our masks and see who was really there, we began to grieve.

With my grief my tears became more about the pain I caused him and myself and our children and friends and God. A shift began to happen in both of us much like the overflow of godly sorrow as described in 2 Corinthians 7 that I previously mentioned.

My grief drew me closer to the One who made me. I collapsed into his merciful embrace and allowed liquid grace to pour from my eyes as he held my heart and soul. Those tears washed away my guilt and my shame and left behind eyes and a heart that could see more clearly God's design for my soul and my life.

What masks are you removing in your grief?

YO TIME AIN'T HER TIME

BEN

*a*fter the revelation, with pretenses stripped away, we had to look at our own sin. I continued my first semester of seminary - barely hanging on. I could do classes like geography that only required memorizing facts and parroting them back. I couldn't manage other classes like New Testament because they required research and bringing together a multitude of ideas into one coherent stream of thought.

I could barely tie my shoes.

Since part of staying together and working on our marriage meant Ann giving up her *sweet* medical sales job, I took a job with FedEx at the airport to make up for lost income. The physical exercise of stacking boxes and loading the large cans on trucks and planes was an excellent steam valve for my anxiety and pain. While working there, I got to know a co-worker named Phyllis.

Phyllis was a tender soul who had been through and was living in hard times. She'd been married to a man whose middle name was Philanderer. On top of that pain her daughter died in an icy car wreck with her other daughter behind the wheel. I hurt just typing this.

Phyllis and I were on the line one night loading a can. I told her my story and told her I dealt with sincere alcoholic suicidal thoughts just before I called to God. With His grace, I slogged through pain and confusion out of the darkness to sobriety and into a newer more reflective life. With regards to the lying and Ann's affair, I said to Phyllis, "I thought we were past all that." I was totally ignoring my own emotional affair, of course.

She looked at me and shared wisdom that only a streetwise person broken on the wheels of living can share.

"Ben, yo time ain't her time."

Yo time ain't her time means I have a journey. Ann has a journey. We have a journey together. Phyllis sounded like Aslan in *A Horse and His Boy*: "Child, I am telling you your story, not hers. I tell no one any story but his own."

I began to grieve how I wounded Ann. I started getting drunk at 13. Ann and I started dating when I was 19. I was well into being an alcoholic by then. I had been with three other women while we dated. We never talked it through. Even if we had talked it through, if my lips were moving I was lying (to quote an AA line about addicts).

I began to see how my emotional affair set Ann up. My eyes opened to the damage I did to my wife's soul by giving my heart to another woman. I left Ann lonely with a sense of rejection. I left her vulnerable to the pursuit of another man.

Prior to the affair, what have been the most significant wounds in your relationship?

ENLARGING OUR SOULS

ANN

The veils slid loose, rustling in the breeze, revealing the truth of what was going on all along. We saw our souls as they really were. Our relationship with God began to deepen. And in more powerful ways, we began to understand... "But whenever anyone turns to the Lord, the veil is taken away. Now the Lord is the Spirit, and where the Spirit of the Lord is, there is freedom. And we, who with unveiled faces all reflect the Lord's glory, are being transformed into his likeness with ever-increasing glory, which comes from the Lord, who is the Spirit" (2 Corinthians 3:16-18 NIV).

As we began to live with unveiled faces, much pain was ours to experience. As we moved through the pain, our souls were enlarged. Enlarging our souls is a term we borrow from Gerald Sittser in *A Grace Disguised* and from Augustine about 1,700 years ago. Augustine led a wild life early on and developed a deep relationship with God later in life. As well as he knew God, he was still completely overwhelmed by the idea of God really loving him.

He said, "My soul is like a house, small for you to enter, but I pray you to enlarge it. It is in ruins, but I ask you to remake it. It contains much that you will not be pleased to see: this I know and do not hide."

During my affair, I continually told myself that even though I knew the affair was wrong, God would forgive me anyway. This not only cheapened God's grace but also hid my pain and my heart from Him and me. A radical shift took place in my prayers after the revelation. They echoed Augustine's prayer. I was in ruins. I was a mess. I felt small. I needed God to overrun my heart and not only remake it but restore its beauty. I quit hiding and started grieving and received His love.

As His restoration caused my soul to enlarge, I not only had more room for my grief, despair and pain, more room also became available for joy, love and grace. The veil of my shallow life no longer offered a cover to hide behind so I began to embrace my pain as the eventual path to my joy and freedom.

Describe the messy state of your soul right now.

GRIEVING THE LOSS
OF YOUR AFFAIR PARTNER

BEN AND ANN

To save my marriage, I was called to challenge myself. I was called to allow my wife to grieve the loss of her affair partner.

It would have been cruel and unusual punishment for me to listen to all that she missed about him and the relationship. I did want to know enough about their affair. My questions involved the who, where, when and why. Thankfully, someone advised me to leave *the what* alone. I didn't want any images about their sexual experiences in my brain. I suffered torture enough knowing they had been sexual. It felt important for me to know: who he was, where they met, if they ever met in our house or in our bed, and what she was receiving at an emotional or soul level from their relationship.

Yet, it was necessary for her to have someone with whom to share the particular loss of her affair partner. For the desire to see him lessen, she needed to voice that he touched something deep within her soul, wrong situation that it was, and that she would miss him and their relationship. By keeping her loss to herself the enemy would have access to twist her good desires much as he did during the affair. By bringing this into the light she could communicate to me aspects of her heart that she wanted me to move towards and touch.

I didn't like this part of the healing process at all. I wanted her to be able to yell, scream and call him a jerk. Even if I thought of him as a jerk at the time, I still had to acknowledge that my wife has exquisite taste and wouldn't choose a man without any redeeming qualities.

My part in this aspect of the grieving process focused on joining with Ann to develop a shared definition of her affair. During the affair, Ann delivered a message to me. I needed to receive that message and make changes in how I treated her.

Our shared definition of the affair included several aspects. Ann appreciated having fun. I had become Mr. Serious Christian, always seeking to be right and moral and forgetting about being dependent on God and having His life-giving grace flow through me. She also wanted to be pursued and romanced. I neglected her and chose not to do this for the most part. I wrongly believed that we needed to have only family time - not romantic time. Ann did not feel I valued her or appreciated her as a woman, as my lover. All of this is central to what she communicated to me by having the affair.

Knowing that she found these important aspects of marriage with another man angered me. I had a choice to make: let my anger become frozen and turn into bitterness or allow my anger to lead me to my hurt, to lead me to looking at my own failures in our marriage. I chose to grieve and repent of my failures, which gave me the freedom to truly pursue my beautiful, glorious bride in the midst of my pain, anger and my desire to forgive.

What was it like for me {Ann} to grieve the loss of Bob? Bob became more than my affair partner; he became a close friend. I looked forward to calls from him, especially when he said he knew he would feel better if he heard my voice. He seemed genuinely interested in my life and me.

But I had so much more to grieve than just the loss of Bob. Certainly, I missed him. I missed the fun we had. I missed the ways he made me feel wanted. But even more than that, I had to grieve what losing him surfaced in my heart.

I had to grieve how stupid I had been. How could I have been drawn in by this smooth-talking salesman? I was. How could I have not seen through all the sticky sweet words he used to build me up? I didn't. I knew what we were doing was wrong from day one, yet I didn't heed the screaming red lights, and I zoomed headlong into a crash just waiting to happen.

I had to grieve being taken advantage of yet again - a replay of my high school years. I would climb into the back seat of a guy's car one night, hoping he might acknowledge me the next day in the halls. Well, that didn't work. It only left me feeling used and lonelier than before.

And I became furious - angry at myself but more angry at Bob. It's like he saw me as an easy mark so he went for it. I was angry that he didn't seem to even care what our relationship did to my marriage or my kids or to his marriage or to his kids. He was just selfish, and I bore the weight of his selfishness.

In the midst of feeling stupidity, anger and loneliness, God began to whisper to my heart. He reminded me that I belong to Him, not Bob. He reminded me that I am beautiful, not ugly. He reminded me that I am loved, not stupid. He bore the weight of my sin. He drew me close with words of grace, love and mercy.

"You did it; you changed wild lament into whirling dance; You ripped off my black mourning band and decked me with wildflowers" (Psalms 30:11-12).

If you haven't started, begin developing the message(s) of this affair. What are the themes, longings and ideas communicated about your marriage via the affair?

BROKEN, LOVED
AND CHANGED

ANN

*P*rior to the affair, my soul remained closed. Very closed. I had shut the door hard, not truly allowing anyone in - not other women, not Ben and certainly not Jesus. Oh, I had *asked Him into my heart*, but I protected certain areas of my soul that I didn't think anyone would want to see, much less spend time there with me. Grieving the affair - the loss of my affair partner, the loss of the illusion of a perfect life, the loss of being a good mom, the loss of being a good wife - certainly cracked that door open a little, but I still guarded it. It could be opened far enough to have chats, but not far enough to allow others to enter and have face-to-face, heart-to-heart conversations.

On one level, I felt okay hiding in my closet. All by myself. But God desired more than me being there. He knew I needed others to join me in my brokenness and grief. The only way to make that happen was to lead me into more brokenness.

Two summers after the revelation of the affair, we decided to move from Missouri to Colorado for Ben to go to graduate school for a counseling degree. It felt like the right decision at the right time. The only thing was, a month before we moved, my dad was diagnosed with stage IV lung cancer. For those of you who don't know what that means, it's not good. It meant his cancer had spread beyond his lungs into his bones, his organs, throughout his body; it meant that he didn't have long to live. Ben offered to put off school for a year, but I felt God asking us - *me* - to trust Him. So Ben purchased a few plane tickets for me to return home to the family cabin and my dying daddy.

In the meantime, in the glorious backdrop of the Denver foothills, I began meeting with other spouses of counseling graduate students. A friend reminded me at the end of the year that I had made the comment at the beginning of the year that "if this group means going beneath the surface, I didn't want to be a part of it because I live on the surface, and I like living on the surface." Yet again, God had a different idea.

During the course of the fall semester, as the aspen trees turned golden and my daddy walked with a cane, as the air became cool and crisp and my daddy required the use of a walker, as the foothills became dusted with snow and my daddy moved to a wheelchair, as the Christmas lights went up and my daddy lay in a hospital bed in his dining room overlooking the wild birds and woods he delighted in, the grief I experienced caused the door to my soul to begin to swing open wide. I began to invite those women in my spouse group into my heart, into the mess that was my soul, my brokenness, my grief. We laughed, we cried. We mourned, we marveled. Consequently, I was broken. I was loved. I was changed.

"We throw open our doors to God and discover at the same moment that he has already thrown open his door to us. We find ourselves standing where we always hoped we might stand—out in the wide open spaces of God's grace and glory, standing tall and shouting our praise" (Romans 5:1-2).

What areas of your heart have you held back from your spouse or others?

SLAYING THE IDOL
OF TRYING TO BE GOOD

BEN

*I*f I was "trying to be good," I would be rebuilding the same old barn that I tore down. I would be acting as a charlatan. (Galatians 2:18).

In the movie *50/50*, Seth Rogen plays Kyle, a vulgar and imperfect but loyal friend. Joseph Gordon-Levitt is Adam, his pal with life-threatening cancer. The night before a defining surgery, Adam takes Kyle's SUV and freaks. He doesn't know how to drive and uses the emergency brake to stop the car and locks the wheels up. As the car yanks to a stop, Adam unleashes an anguished scream/groan as the weight of his life smashes through to reality. This scream is the closest thing I have heard since the day I let out my own scream after Ann revealed her affair.

Ann told me about her affair on a Tuesday afternoon. On Wednesday, with her sitting by my side, I called the pastor at my home church to let him know I wouldn't be home on Sunday to preach my first scheduled service. As I placed the receiver down, sounds from my depths erupted. Guttural sobs bellowed forth tasting like acidic raw sorrow. To her credit and courage, Ann sat by my side.

After several minutes, the words "I was finally going to be something good" came out. Trying *to be good* had become an idol to me. It was all about me, not me being dependent on God. So my grief was a mix of authentic, honest pain and groans and also the beginning of the slaying of an idol. Though subtle, I wanted to be good more than I wanted to know God. I was broken by Ann's affair and broken by my own idolatry.

My soul expanded in my grief.

I also learned about grieving daily. Each time the sun came up I felt the betrayal of the affair. I learned that even without the pain of an affair, loss and pain lead to grief each and every day on this fallen planet. Life isn't right here - a freeing thought for me. I realized I wasn't crazy because I wasn't happy and peppy all the time. It's not wrong to allow myself a place to feel sorrow over loss. It's not a question of whether loss exists. It does. The question becomes do I choose to deal with it or numb it?

We were designed for heaven. Reality is much less than the glory that awaits us leaving a huge gap between that design and reality. I've been creative in my methods to fill it. These were idols as well: alcohol, golf, trying to be cool, trying to be quiet, serving at church, reading the Bible, working extra hours on weekends, on and on.

But God rigged the world. We can really only fill the gap with grief. That's it. Acknowledging this isn't our real home and experiencing loss is one way to define grief. The amazing thing is God meets us - in our grief, in that gap, and pours His grace. Grief and grace bridge the disparity between the original design of our world and the reality we live in.

In grieving, I eventually could enjoy the beauty that Ann brings into my life. Grief purified and expanded my soul to relax and enjoy who she was becoming and all the ways she already blessed my life.

Grief is like Kyle. It's a vulgar, imperfect, loyal friend. It's a friend that penetrates our depths leading us to guttural screams and sobs and groans. God *eventually* meets us at the deep intersection of truth and life filling us with his grace. *Eventually* can seem like it will never get here.

"Meanwhile, the moment we get tired in the waiting, God's Spirit is right alongside helping us along. If we don't know how or what to pray, it doesn't matter. He does our praying in and for us, making prayer out of our wordless sighs, our aching groans. He knows us far better than we know ourselves, knows our pregnant condition, and keeps us present before God" (Romans 8:26-27).

How have you expressed your deepest anguish about the affair?

STRAIGHT UP-
NOT SHAKEN, NOT STIRRED

BEN

Grief strips away the pretenses of our lives and enlarges our souls. Grief also facilitates our knowing more of God.

Deep trust is realized through Christ and through suffering. Moving towards Christ in our suffering allows us to see God as bigger than our pain and helps us trust Him more. When we trust God's goodness, we can make choices to stay in pain and to forgive and reconcile relationships.

Essentially, we know God more if we allow ourselves to hurt and be honest with God about it.

God knows grief because He grieved. I've heard it said there is really only one sermon in the Old Testament. The Israelites are close to God and are blessed. They get comfortable and forget God brings the good in their lives, and they begin to slide away. God hurts, life gets worse, and eventually God pursues them with mercy until they return to Him. The world isn't totally the same with the New Testament of

Christ, but in many ways we do the same thing as the Israelites.

Psalms of lament illustrate this truth of knowing God more fully as we go through pain and grief.

> "How long, O Lord? Will you forget me forever?
> How long will you hide your face from me?
> How long must I wrestle with my thoughts and every day have sorrow in my heart?
> How long will my enemy triumph over me?
> Look on me and answer, O Lord my God.
> Give light to my eyes, or I will sleep in death;
> my enemy will say, "I have overcome him,'
> and my foes will rejoice when I fall.
> But I trust in your unfailing love; my heart rejoices in your salvation
> I will sing to the Lord, for he has been good to me."
> (Psalm 13 NIV).

The Bible is honest, straight up - not shaken, not stirred. It deals with every raw emotion and situation ever experienced by humankind. The following is my summary of a lament psalm like the one above, which follows the pattern of many lament Psalms:

Life sucks . . . Where are you God? . . . I still believe in you.

If you connect with Psalm 13 and others like it you are in good company. I encourage you to pray it and pray it and pray it again. Wrestle in the midst of your sorrow. Seek His answer. And even though the circumstances of your life may lead you to experience God as untrustworthy, take the next step into the mystery doing your best to trust in His unfailing love.

Where do you connect with Psalm 13? It is a powerful exercise to write your own psalm and I encourage you to do so.

GOD DOESN'T PROMISE LESS PAIN

BEN AND ANN

*I*f you have stayed with us this far while dealing with the shock of an affair, we admire your courage. This process is full of low lows and high highs with enough pain to fill Mile High Stadium.

Oddly enough, in some ways you may feel closer to your spouse than you have in a while *if* you've been talking and talking and talking about everything. There can be moments of deep connection while sorting through the betrayal, the lies and the deception. Your masks are removed, and honesty emerges.

It could be the first time in years that you are looking, really looking, into each other's eyes to see what's inside.

Perhaps you've battled suicidal thoughts. If so, we're glad you are still alive. If you are considering taking your life, tell someone right now. We can promise you the pain will decrease at some point. Life will be rich again, but it will take time.

The early days can be a living hell: lack of sleep, a home filled with a constant mist of tension resting on your skin, and an anvil for your chest waiting to press in on your lungs each morning when you awake. Some days you have to scream the f-word for 10 seconds to ease the pain for a moment - a little *King's Speech* therapy, if you will.

Wrestle with God. Take your big questions to Him. We were filled with worship and doubts. We felt Him close, and felt betrayed by Him for all the pain we were facing. We learned later He never promised a life of less pain. Our hearts hurt. Yet we found out that He did not waste an ounce of our pain.

So we say congratulations. You are a man or woman of great courage and perseverance. This deal is going to be harder and last longer than you want. Every day, part of you will want to get out. That's normal. Every day, part of you will want to stay and latch on to any piece of hope or light that says somehow your marriage will survive this and be even better. That's normal, too.

It's a wild ride. The lows will indeed be low, and the highs will indeed be high; but in the end we believe you'll be glad you stayed on for the whole trek. Our experience leads us to believe that navigating through the pain brings rich rewards.

What is most difficult for you today? Most hopeful?

LAUGH HEARTILY, SHARE SORROW

BEN

When dealing with an affair, a couple might experience a shift in friendships. Often, friends you enjoyed spending great times with suddenly don't want to be around you and the tension. Other friends on the fringe before now seem to move toward you and/or your spouse.

Isolation waits to pounce. Isolation whispers believable lies:

"Nobody wants to deal with your pain."

"Your anger is too volatile for anyone to enjoy being with you."

"You're a mess, and nobody wants to be with a mess."

Don't withdraw from friendships due to shame and guilt over difficulty in your marriage. Shame likes to isolate. Two poor ways we handle this emotion are to truly disengage and stay away from others or we live behind a facade so no one can really get close. The facade has to go! Honesty is a must! Resist the temptation to distance yourself from others. Mature friends can handle you in your messiness. During this transitional time, intentionally seek out a person or two or three to regularly connect with who can handle your pain, your anger, your messiness and who also have a listening ear for God.

What traits will these friends have? They'll value authenticity, wanting to get the real you, not the facade. They'll be able to cry with you in your sorrow. They'll be able to stay with you when you share your anger - even if it is loud and a little (or a lot) over the top. They won't walk on eggshells but will instead feel the freedom to crack a joke and laugh heartily with you. Also, these friends will listen well to your heart. Most importantly, they won't try to fix you through offering cheap advice that comes out of their own uncomfortable reaction to your pain and anger.

These extra eyes and ears will help you see your relationship more clearly. They can help you sort through your behaviors, feelings and thoughts. They'll sense a good time to talk more about God and spiritual matters and know when to come in through another door.

As time goes on, you should lean less on your friends and more on your mate during this messy, rocky process. These friends can help you stay sane in the craziness of affair recovery. Even so, the greater friendship goal is learning to express your heart, including your anger, with your spouse. This expression comes in a way that builds your marriage up not tear it down.

So stay in relationship with those who are for you and for your marriage. It's a long journey, and we all need compassionate friends to prop us up or say a kind (or even a difficult) word. Sometimes we just need a breathing friend to sit in the same room while God has His way with our soul.

Who are your friends that you trust with all of you, good and bad? If you don't have anyone, where can you begin that search?

GRIEVING IN A CULTURE THAT DOESN'T GRIEVE WELL

BEN

Most work places give you three days to grieve a death. They provide a day to travel, a day for the funeral, and a day for return travel. Then get over it, and get back to work. Soul truncation.

Our culture doesn't grieve well, so most of us end up stuck in our pain. My stomach churns when I see a shallow list, a get-rid-of-pain quick list, instructing people to get over grief like an illness. Get busy always appears on these lists. Keep doing. Distract yourself. Don't honor the depth of your love. That's how one heals. Ugh!

Grieving is not depression. Grieving is grieving. You don't need to take a pill when grief weighs down your soul. Sadness is not a sin. Sadness is acknowledging that something sad happened - like an affair that flipped your life upside down.

Grieving your losses grows one's soul.
Grieving grows our capacity to love.

Grieving signifies a sign of strength not weakness.

Our friend, Krista, penned these words on strength and grieving. "While shopping for a sympathy card today I was amazed at the amount of cards that wished the grieving person 'STRENGTH' in his or her time of loss. Living in our society, to me this says 'wishing you the ability to go on like nothing ever happened, to keep your eyes dry, to not make anyone else too uncomfortable, and certainly to not *feel* anything.'"

Krista suggests an alternative card for those who grieve:

"Wishing you TRUE STRENGTH in this time of loss.
The STRENGTH it takes to be vulnerable.
The STRENGTH it takes to allow yourself to cry.
The STRENGTH it takes to enter into the incredibly painful grieving process.
The STRENGTH that comes with the courage to question the meaning of life and suffering and loss.
The STRENGTH it takes to ask friends for help because you're overwhelmed with the pain.
The STRENGTH it takes to allow yourself to stay in bed or miss work or not clean the house.
The STRENGTH it takes to question God's goodness.
And the STRENGTH it takes to allow yourself to melt like a puddle on your kitchen floor because you simply don't know what else to do.

Today I wish you that STRENGTH, and when you run out, I offer you mine - not in doing for you or taking care of you - but in grieving with you."

Grieving with you. That's where we hope you are headed as a couple - being *with* one another in your grief, having compassion for the other on a hard day, picking up the slack for each other when your energy hides under the carpet.

Grieving together honors the depth of love in your marriage. It will eventually help you discover an even deeper love.

Find something to grieve about as a couple rather than individually. What can you sorrow over together, together being the important part?

A BEAUTIFUL, PAINFUL MYSTERY

BEN AND ANN

*P*ain and loss are inevitable guests in our lives, yet we resist, and our refusal to grieve causes many problems throughout life. Children are taught not to grieve in different ways. "Don't cry or I'll give you something to cry about!" "You're such a big baby!" "Be strong, don't let it bother you." More extreme examples exist when a child grows up in an addictive or abusive home.

Poet and novelist Rainer Maria Rilke said, "Once the realization is accepted that even between the closest human beings infinite distance must continue to exist, a wonderful living side by side can grow up." He illustrates our tendency to use people to fill holes in our soul that really can't be filled here. We live in a fallen world with fallen people. Where people are fallen, there is pain.

But we want Heaven now, understandably, because we were created for Heaven. The reality is we don't have it now. Tension surfaces as we are created for perfect bliss and contentment but live in a place that delivers far less. We're left with a gap. We mentioned this gap earlier, but let's explore it more fully.

We ask what we can fill the gap with. We hear the do good and work harder responses of more Bible study, helping the homeless, walking an elderly woman across the street. In fact, people do try to fill the gap doing good things. These activities have value except when used to fill the gap, resulting in soul-numbing busyness.

Churches sometimes promote gap-filling busyness by looking for those who know how to get things done, people like Ann. Before the affair, a few months after returning to church, she taught Sunday School, sang in the choir, helped with the youth group and more. On top of all that she worked full-time, served as a Girl Scout leader and chauffeured our children to their plethora of activities.

She couldn't say no, and leaders in the church and elsewhere continually asked her to do more. God seemingly orchestrated the blowout from the affair to get Ann to stop and meet Him in the gap.

Relationships are another way we fill the gap. Ben's emotional affair was a way of seeking a human drug to do away with the uncomfortable feelings on this earth. Without realizing it he was demanding that I make life heaven now which is impossible as I'm only a woman and we're not there – we're here. So in his sin he sought relief from the gap.

We also try to fill it with substances. We get drunk, high or wasted to numb the gap momentarily. In our culture, we slam down massive amounts of sugar and processed foods to numb emotional pain. Ben has battled this most of his life, growing up on vending machine cinnamon rolls and cans of Mountain Dew at the golf course.

Oh, we're ingenious in the ways we attempt to feel like we are in Heaven now. There is much to be grateful for here, but we are still here and not there. So what can we put in the gap? Anything?

We can groan. We can repent of refusing to grieve and then grieve. We can experience this world with both eyes open. We can take in the glorious and take in the terrible. We can sorrow. We can ache over the state of pain and loss on this planet. That doesn't mean we can't act to alleviate some of it, but that is beneath the gap. So we can groan, grieve and sorrow. However we say it, we can own that we don't live in a perfect place.

As we groan and face the gap honestly, grace is poured in. Groaning and grace exist in the gap; yet grace doesn't eliminate the groaning. We hurt, and in our hurt we experience God's love. It's a mysterious place. When we allow the mystery to be, it is a place of incredible spiritual formation and transformation. We let God be God. Yahweh.

When a couple dealing with an affair can grieve side by side they will encounter God's grace together. It's a mystery. A beautiful, painful mystery.

"Creation groans, the people of God groan, and the Holy Spirit groans. What's the connection? We groan because of sins effects upon us. The Spirit groans in prayer in order to identify with our groanings, deliver them to God, and deliver to us from God what we need to be sustained in a world that produces pain." ~Pastor and Author Tony Evans

What have you put in the gap? How have you placed your spouse there?

DESPAIR
AS A PATHWAY TO GRACE

BEN

As a counselor, 75 percent of what I do is encourage others to grieve. It's a weird job. Fortunately, I also urge people to celebrate, play and appreciate beauty.

As clients begin therapy, most want kitsch. Kitsch is the absence of shit. It's little chubby-cheeked angels and playful kittens; kitsch contains the depth of a promise from a checkered coat-wearing used car salesman.

Kitsch isn't what theologian Lewis Smedes offers in his book on forgiveness. In *The Art of Forgiving*, Smedes says, "Despair, like hell, is where we experience the absence of God. However, in the very place we feel most desolate, He can find us, and when He does, we will know for sure He comes with grace."

We experience despair when we own the damage our sin causes loved ones. At first, it's tempting to totally hide from our own sin, thus avoiding despair. "Maybe no one will know and no one will be hurt."

After the exposure of sin the temptation is quick forgiveness. "I'm sorry I did that. Please forgive me. Let's don't talk about it and move on." But real healing often means encountering despair. We encounter despair after hearing and experiencing the pain our sin caused loved ones. This is expressed like this: "I sinned against you. Tell me about your pain and what it was like for you?" Facing the pain we cause in the eyes of those we wound can lead to despair. Despair emerges as our depravity feels deeper than imagined.

This despair can seem like a never-ending darkened path. We experience abandonment, but it isn't really abandonment. In our darkness the lie that I will never be loved seems quite true. The hope of redemption seems like a fantasy for those in another world. But God loves to surprise. As we face the pain our sin causes, God loves us lavishly. Such a beautiful paradox.

Our honesty brings new light onto our darkened path as does our courage in facing life straight up. To be honest with God and others there has to be a sense of trust and surrender. One may not even be aware of this trust at first. In my opinion, God loves to be trusted. And when He is trusted we somehow experience more of his Grace.

Ponder David's words after his affair with Bathsheba was exposed.

> "Count yourself lucky, how happy you must be—
> you get a fresh start, your slate's wiped clean.
> Count yourself lucky—
> God holds nothing against you
> and you're holding nothing back from him.

When I kept it all inside,
my bones turned to powder,
my words became daylong groans.
The pressure never let up;
all the juices of my life dried up.
Then I let it all out;
said, "I'll make a clean breast of my failures
to God."
Suddenly the pressure was gone—
my guilt dissolved,
my sin disappeared"
(Psalm 32:1-6).

For over nine months, David concealed his sin of adultery and murder. He denied the damage he perpetrated on those he loved and those he used. Do you connect with his daylong groans? How about the pressure of carrying lies around? David suffered in a place of despair.

You may be in a place of despair today. The way out is honesty with God, honesty with those you've wounded and listening to the pain you've caused them. It's a hard, dark path. The path will be longer than you want. But it is only so long - not infinite. And know for sure that God will find you, and He will come with Grace.

How have you wounded your spouse? Be specific.

GRIEF IS A MESSY RIDE

ANN

I returned to work after a trip to southern Missouri where the rocky, rolling Ozark hills contain my family's land. Being there always stirs warm memories of my dad. He was a constant putzer. He didn't move too quickly in his overalls, but he was always working on the garden, planting a tree, tending the hogs (named "Ham," "Bacon," "Babe" and "Wilbur"), mending the chicken coop or sorting the latest-and-greatest auction finds.

Later, as I recalled these fond images, tears created pathways down my cheeks. A co-worker asked what was going on and I recounted the memories, missing my dad. In a mood that implied she didn't think he died too long ago, my friend asked when he had passed. I replied, "Over fifteen years ago."

Grieving is tough to grasp for the rational-minded person. Shoot, it's tough for anyone to *get grief* and move through it. Grieving *as a couple* over an affair can't be planned out, but it must happen. At first, grief feels like a constant unwelcome guest; later grief becomes a darting sprite here and gone in unexpected moments.

Given that, we want to share a few common aspects of grief, though no two journeys through grief are the same.

Unpredictable and random, grief knows no master. Those who think they have it mastered will discover physical problems like ulcers and other indicators like anxiety or irritability. Grief comes when it comes. Hurt crashes in at unpredictable times. It caught Ben off guard the first wedding we attended after the revelation. Four years had passed. We had healed and healed and healed some more. But when Ben heard the vows at this wedding, the promises of dedication and fidelity, an invisible sword sliced into his soul reminding him of our infidelities.

Along with being unpredictable, grief can be a messy and out-of-control adventure. It arrives like an uninvited dinner guest, unpredictable in timing and intensity. Grief might hit you when walking through the household department at Target, shopping for a basic necessity. It slams you with a painful reminder (maybe triggered by the laundry detergent used in earlier, happier times) causing tears and snot to fly in aisle six. Grief is humbling in its messiness.

Along with this, grief is disruptive. A new normal is being formed, and grief makes sure normal doesn't become normal too soon. Crying during a basketball game, or being struck dumb because you just walked by a person wearing your affair partner's cologne or perfume and you hadn't thought of him or her in a while - seemingly, grief throws you backward unexpectedly. In reality, we underestimate the amount of pain that sorrow requires.

Grief doesn't follow a direct route. It's a two-lane highway on a crooked, winding ridge. Three-easy-steps grief plans don't take into account road construction, accidents, vehicle malfunctions and snowstorms like the ones in Colorado where highways are shut down. Grief winds and turns daily, but rarely are there dangerous curves ahead signs.

Grief also lasts longer than expected. We encourage you to reflect and see if you have been grieving together. Losses need to be faced. Perhaps that's today or maybe it will be years down the road like me grieving my dad.

What has unexpectedly brought tears to your eyes?

CHOOSING TO LOVE AGAIN

BEN AND ANN

e experienced real pain, soul trauma, with the revelation of the affair. The pain is often the most intense pain to ever be encountered (at least it was for us). You might think it will be more prudent to play it safe, be buds, keep the majority of the benefits of marriage, but not put your heart out there because you never want that soul explosion ripping up your insides again. That seems to be the safer way.

But safety is an illusion. No matter what, there is always risk; and we put our hearts at great risk when we choose not to love. C.S. Lewis said it this way: "To love at all is to be vulnerable. Love anything, and your heart will certainly be wrung and possibly be broken. If you want to make sure of keeping it intact, you must give your heart to no one, not even to an animal. Wrap it carefully round with hobbies and little luxuries; avoid all entanglements; lock it up safe in the casket or coffin of your selfishness. But in that casket — safe, dark, motionless, airless — it will change. It will not be broken; it will become unbreakable, impenetrable, irredeemable."

Now that's a risk. Not loving again puts our hearts in danger of becoming cold iron. Nothing gets in but nothing comes out either. Comparing it to our physical heart, nothing gets pumped in and nothing shoots back out taking life to our limbs.

In the early stages of affair recovery loving again can feel impossible. It's that level of impossibility that makes love regained miraculous. It will take trusting God to choose to love again. It's almost like we need to trust Love, with a capital L, before we can love again.

Reopening our hearts to love again is scary, even while trusting God. Fresh wounds get exposed and become vulnerable. It may even seem masochistic to choose to love again. Yet, at the end of this journey we have a much greater capacity to give and receive love.

For God to redeem the pain of betrayal there must be a choice to grieve and eventually make a choice to love even more than before. It's the spirit's finest work of alchemy. The Holy Spirit takes the common scrap metal resulting from the affair, and through grieving and choosing to love again transforms the heap into sky illuminating gold.

What thoughts and emotions are stirred when you ponder loving again?

AM I A MISTAKE?

An affair brings many questions. Most view an affair as wrong. It's in the Ten Commandments. Right there at number seven we are told do not commit adultery. Questioning *did I make a mistake* isn't necessary. But other questions have the potential to lead us in good directions. So if it is wrong and I am generally a truthful person how did I end up in an affair? What led me down this path? Why didn't God stop me?

Other questions lead towards the searing isolation of shame. What is wrong with me? Am I defective? Am I a mistake? Shame sticks to our soul like super glue when we explore these questions. These shame questions, and others, lead to damaging answers. God screwed up making me. I better be perfect or I'll never know love. If others really knew me they'd want nothing to do with me. I'm so messed up there is no hope.

There is hope. Shame is a tough old bird, but healing is possible. Healing requires exposing your shame questions and answers to others and God. In this vulnerability, in facing your fears of rejection, you will face another question. Do I have the courage to receive from the Grace-Giver?

SURPRISED BY REDEMPTION

BEN

On my blog I once quoted a sermon from author and pastor Peter Hiett. Here's an excerpt from the blog post called "Did Jesus Come Just to Kick Your Ass?"

"So I'm convinced your deepest problem is not the cigarettes you smoke or the alcohol you drink in secret. It's not the slander you speak and the gossip you cherish. It's not the pornography you pleasure yourself with when no one's looking. It's not the baby you aborted; it's not that you betrayed your brother, cheated on your bride, lied about the whole thing . . . It's not even that you slaughtered the Lamb and killed the Messiah. Your deepest problem is that somewhere deep down inside, you believe Jesus the Messiah rose from the dead just to kick your ass, when, in fact, He rose from the dead so you would believe all is forgiven. It is finished! Justice is accomplished. And the Father is pleading, 'Come home, come home, come home!'"

A reader took offense to my post. He left me this query:

"I'm not sure what Hiett is talking about. Pardon my ignorance here. And whatever he's talking about,

I'm not seeing the necessity to use profanity to make the point. Could anyone explain?"

My response was, "Beats the hell out of me!"

Actually, I'm just kidding. Hiett is trying to say that most of us are afraid of God. We consider our sin the biggest deal, but our biggest problem is that we won't receive the grace and tenderness of our God. He's not saying sin isn't an issue but that we can get lost in worry, guilt and shame and miss out on the stupendous, radical love of God because we see him as a stern, cold disciplinarian and not Abba, a loving father.

The use of the word ass instead of buttocks or rear end was probably a little for shock value but also it helped people get past their church face and get in touch with their underlying guilt and shame. An antidote for shame is acceptance – one aspect of grace. God accepts us even in our heinous sin (Romans 5:8), but that isn't the present reality for most of us.

For the longest time I lived with an unhealthy fear of God. I forgot just how afraid I was until I had dinner recently with my college roommate, Stan.

Stan and his family came to town, so we gathered our kids and went out to dinner. As we chatted about college life and God, Stan remembered thinking that I was coming to God on my own time.

I attended church once or twice with Stan in high school when I visited him to play golf. But in college I never attended church with him.

At dinner, Stan recalled asking me to go on one occasion. He said I replied, "Stan, I know I need to go.

I am just not ready to feel that bad about everything I'm doing." We all busted out laughing.

God sure has me now.

The irony is as I kept God at bay I really felt worse and worse. Several years after I lived with Stan I eventually became suicidal. Talk about feeling bad!

I am reminded that in all my time of truly being in relationship with God and the light of His Love He has never made me feel bad. I may have felt shame, guilt or sorrow because *I* turned my back on Him, but that's expected in any relationship when you hurt someone you dearly love.

How often we forget St. Paul's words that we sing in church; it is God's kindness that leads us to repentance. God is kind. He is about redemption, grace and love. He didn't kick my ass. He brought me home to be with Him and to have a party.

How do you view God? Is He a stern, cold disciplinarian, or Abba, a loving Father? What events do you believe shaped your view?

YOU ARE NOT A MISTAKE

ANN

Guilt says I *made* a mistake. Shame says I *am* a mistake.

Did I feel guilt over my affair? You betcha. I knew I was making a mistake by being in the bed of another. I remember the voice of guilt rising only to be quieted by my selfish voice saying "It's okay. God will forgive you." What a way to cheapen God's grace.

Then shame began to rise in my soul. Rather than sorrow over the guilt of my hideous choices, I began to hide and believe the lies that I had zero value and zero grace. You see, the root of the word shame means *to cover*. So I hid my exposed ugliness. I didn't want others to see my soul that was now covered in the dust, dirt and mud of the trashy road I'd been traveling. I backed out of responsibilities. I would duck in and out of church only long enough to say I'd been there, not truly to worship. I stayed home every chance I could, unusual for my extroverted self. I wore clothes two sizes too big so no one would notice my figure or me. My hiding gave shame plenty of room to attack my soul at the core of my being.

Shame began to whisper that I was a failure. "What have you done? You've screwed up your life. No one will believe your testimony now."

Shame began to tell me that I was inadequate. "You'll never be able to make this right. You couldn't even get it right to begin with. Why even try?"

Shame began to shout that I was worthless. "You are lower than dirt. You are no longer worthy to be called a daughter of God."

Shame began to scream that I was unlovable. "Ben will never love you again. Your kids will never love you again. God will never love you again."

Have you heard those voices? Have you listened to them? Have you believed them? Me too. I believed them for far too long. They were like the shady characters hanging out on the side of that trashy road just waiting to attack. And attack they did. They delighted in robbing me of dignity, hope and any semblance of trust. I didn't trust others. I certainly didn't trust myself. I made hideous choices. And I wasn't quite sure I trusted God. Why didn't he drag me off that trashy road sooner?

The answer has less to do with Him and more to do with me. I was unwilling for too many years to stay in His grip. I would wriggle free every chance I got, uncomfortable in His grip of Grace. Oh, His precious embrace wasn't suffocating or too tight. I just wasn't able to surrender my soul to the One who made it.

How have you hidden, past and present, as a result of your shame? What lies do you hear from shame?

HIDING UNDER OUR SHAME

ANN

"Ready or not, here I come!" Those words end the countdown in Hide and Seek, the familiar childhood game. As a person caught up in shame, you can bet that I learned to *always* be 'ready,' always well hidden. I did not want to be found. Remember, I didn't trust so I hid, especially my heart. I hid from others, and I hid from God.

Hiding our hearts disallows us from being known. It's not just the ugly bits we hide but the beautiful ones as well. As we hide in our shame, we become unwilling to believe and accept the truth of who we are as God's sons and daughters, so we give Satan power. Then, Satan uses that power to access the wounds of our past and he attempts to wound us repeatedly in those same places. In our weakened state, we believe his lies of condemnation and feel the urge to hide even more.

Continued hiding keeps us in the grip of shame instead of in the grip of Grace. Satan knows the power of the embrace of the One who loves us, who gives us the good gift of hope. He revels in the fact that our hiding keeps us in his tight-fisted grasp with little hope. Locking us in the shame of our past is one of his favorite objectives. He knows that when we lock up our hearts tight, shame feels like death, so we close the door not only to Grace but also to life.

Many times, the wounds of our past emerge as themes in our lives. Those themes can frequently be painful, but they are also powerful. When we spend time to gain insight and recognize themes of our past, God reframes these wounds and diffuses their power and our shame. This gives Satan fewer wounds to pierce with his prickly weapons of fear and destruction.

Sexual sin is a theme in my family story. I don't have space to go into details, but suffice it to say sexual sin has impacted me and each of my siblings in significant ways. As I have opened the door to Grace, I now understand some of my life realities that made me vulnerable and led to dreadful decisions.

I no longer hide where I've been and what I've done, even the scandalous things. "Ready or not" has a different ring these days. I am always ready these days, too, but not by hiding. Readiness these days comes as I open my heart and remember. Remembering God's redemption of my story keeps my heart vibrantly alive. *My* story isn't really my story anyway. It's His story of Grace and redemption - redemption of me, my heart, my life.

"We can't just put our pasts behind us. We've got to put our pasts in front of God. He longs to reframe our pasts and let us see them against the backdrop of His glory. Never ever forget that our God is a redeemer."

~BETH MOORE

What wounds have pricked and pierced your soul? Do you see any themes emerge as you explore your wounds?

REDEMPTION IS RISKY

ANN

Redemption is risky business yet absolutely worth every ounce of risk required. What am I risking, you ask? I risk revealing myself. I risk speaking truth. I risk knowing myself. I risk acceptance, and, most of all, I risk love.

My friend, Sara, likes to say, "Shame that is spoken is broken." Those words resonate deeply in my soul as I have come to believe that only revealed shame can be healed. This belief is not only founded in my own healing and that of others I have witnessed, it is supported by author Dr. Brené Brown's research in the area of shame and vulnerability. She has found that "shame hates having words wrapped around it" and that "language and story bring light to shame and destroys it."

I gain strength and courage every time I share my story. Yet, one of the first times I publically shared my story to a large group of women, initially my vulnerability was feared. The woman who invited me to speak was a little hesitant that I share *all* of my story, including my affair. "Women can be cruel," she said. I stood firm in my belief that to share only the bright and shiny parts of my story would be an incomplete story. It would omit the glory of God's redemptive story woven into mine as I experienced healing. Well, ya know what? Not one of those few hundred women was cruel. Turns out, wrapping words around my shame not only helped to destroy my own shame but also gave other women courage to begin to wrap words around their shame.

In order to know my story and strangle shame with words, I had to know the truth of my story. I used to read John 8:32 and think it was a warm fuzzy verse about salvation. That's only part of the story. It reads, "You will know the truth, and the truth will set you free." I have learned these few words address so much more than just my eternal soul. Shame may be powerful, but Truth is extravagantly more powerful in its capacity to redeem. My healing would only go as deep as I was willing to look; so I began to access the deepest parts of my soul where truth, as well as pain, resides. The problem was I had difficulty discerning fact from fiction because of the years I had covered that truth with lies designed to make life hurt less. With a lot of help from counselors, friends and Ben, I learned to be honest and open with myself. This led to an ability to clearly sift through what was true and what was not true in my life and in my story.

Then came the hard part. Yep, you guessed it. I revealed the truth - not just to myself, not just to God but also to anyone who came across my path. I was pretty sure that God loved me in the midst of all that pain and truth, but other people? I wasn't so sure about them. Remember, people can be cruel. I experienced that cruelty growing up. I felt less than. I was the butt of far too many jokes. I was used and abused by those who just wanted more. Maybe I would be better off just hanging out with God and not risking the rejection of those crowds around me.

"But wait," God said. "If you stay only with me, how will others know of my Love? How will they know how lavishly I've poured Love on you and how much I want to pour Love on them?" So I listened to Truth. I listened to Grace. I listened to Love. As I listened, I got to know my heart - a rich reward. I now reveal that heart, my *whole* heart, the dark places, too. I speak truth even when it's hard. I seek out relationships, and fight to keep them. And most of all, I find myself in the midst of more Love than I ever dreamed could be mine.

What words define your shame? What healing words can you wrap around your shame? Find a safe friend, counselor or group of friends to share them with.

BROKENNESS:
AN ANTIDOTE TO SHAME

ANN

We don't usually think of being broken as a powerful state. Author and therapist Dan Allender says that "brokenness is an antidote to shame." An antidote is powerful indeed as it is defined as "anything that counteracts or relieves a harmful or unwanted condition." I know of few conditions more harmful or unwanted than shame. In the case of shame, brokenness carries great power.

What exactly is brokenness? What does it look and feel like? I found myself face down on the floor unable to move or speak. My heart felt as though it weighed two tons, full of shame and the horror of what I had done. My eyes dared not look at the One who loved me and who had the power to lift me up out of the heap of bones that lay on the floor.

Gratefully, Christ looks past our sin and shame to our brokenness. He saw the way of lies and deceit I walked. But then He looked past that path to the broken mourning and wailing of my heavy heart. He heard my brokenness even when I couldn't utter a word. He saw a humble heart that knew it was no longer worthy of His love. He then did what He always does. He poured Grace.

When we are broken, when we have these gaping cracks in our souls; this Grace He pours has greater access to all the darkness, filth and pain. So while you may think that those huge chasms are something to cover and close, these are the gaps where Grace finds its way in.

As Grace seeps into every fracture in our souls, we begin to gain strength. Not strength of the usual kind. This is the strength found only through the power of brokenness. It is not strength that can hoist the world on its shoulders; instead, it is strength that can lift my broken soul from the soil and give it the courage to move and to speak. It is not strength that can throw stack upon stack of stones; it is strength that can cast the heaviness of my heart aside. It is not the strength that adds muscle to my frame; rather, it is strength that held me in a tender embrace as I began to gaze into the eyes of the Lover of my soul.

What does your brokenness look and feel like for you?

ME TOO

ANN

"You too? I thought I was the only one." If I could count the number of times I have heard this phrase from women in groups I have led, I would be counting long into next week. Women share their trauma, their pain, their longings, their desires and thus gain assurance from others that they are not alone. Many common experiences exist that connect women to each other. We just have to muster up the courage to reveal them.

As I mentioned in a previous entry, shame thrives on secret keeping. But as shame researcher Brené Brown says, "Shame is a social concept - it happens between people - and also heals best between people." If we can connect to one another in the midst of our shame, pain and trauma, we can also experience healing in the midst of our shame, pain and trauma.

I like to call part of this healing the Me Too Principle. When I share my story of adultery and shame, it is rare that a woman doesn't come to me after and essentially say, "Me too." She may not use those words, but she always thanks me for being bold enough to speak what she hasn't been able to. In many ways, connecting through our stories gives her hope that she is not the only one attempting to erase the scarlet letter from her soul. She now knows that someone else understands her story, her pain and her shame.

Empathy takes place when we gain the strength to be authentic with our stories and our lives. If you're not familiar with empathy, it is the ability to understand and share someone else's feelings. It is the ability to say "Me too" when you hear another's story because you've been there. You can identify with and understand the shame, pain and trauma. And let me tell you this: shame hates empathy. Since shame despises empathy, shame and empathy cannot coexist.

Shame loathes empathy as it connects us to one another. Where shame attempts to isolate, empathy solidly connects. When we listen to another share their pain, shame loses its grip on their soul. Accepting another's story without judgment speaks volumes to that individual of their worth and value, unlike shame that speaks to them of their insignificance and inferiority.

We essentially communicate to one another a powerful message: "You're not alone. You're not the only one." You no longer have to hide under your shame. You no longer have to fear total rejection. You no longer have to wonder if others think your soul is ugly. You can join me in saying "Me, too." I have hidden. I have feared. I have wondered. No longer. As long as we stay connected, shame cannot live in our hearts. So, my friend, stay connected. Stay connected.

Ponder a time when you've been able to say "Me too." Describe what that was like for you. Who are those you connect with today? What will it take to stay connected with them during this dark time in your life?

SHAME IS A TOUGH OLD BIRD

ANN

I've just returned from a missed breakfast with a new friend from church. Missed because I misread my appointment reminder. Totally my fault. As I stepped out of my car to head into the restaurant I checked my calendar and stopped in my tracks when it said 8:30. You see, it was 9:30.

I called and left a message apologizing immediately. Then I sent an apologetic email. I am hopeful we will still get a chance to break bread together. Now I fight the shame welling up in my soul because I left this new friend hanging at the restaurant.

You see, shame is a tough old bird and she just won't leave me be. She got her claws in me pretty deep after my affair was revealed, and I keep throwing her off; yet she keeps settling back on. My soul is pocked with her claw marks, mostly healed over, but every now and then she reminds me of her powerful presence and how she enjoys seeing me shrivel in my shame.

But shriveled I won't stay because a more powerful presence has settled on my soul - more powerful than that foul-feathered fiend called shame. It is Grace. Grace gives me the courage to call my friend and apologize. Grace gives me the strength to toss off that tough old bird. She is not welcome. She will not stay.

She is no longer welcome because Grace has come to stay, and Grace leaves no space for her to roost. And even though shame causes me to fear rejection and disconnection, Grace offers me the one thing I need most: the gift of being accepted *before* I become acceptable. Grace looks at my ugliness (my forgetfulness, my clumsiness, my haughtiness) and embraces me in the midst of it. So even if my new friend doesn't return my text, or my call, or my email, I do not have to succumb to shame. Rather, I will give in to Grace. Beautiful Grace.

What is your experience with the tenacity of that tough old bird, shame? What will be required of you to surrender to Grace?

HOW CAN I
TRUST YOU AGAIN?

*D*ishonesty: that's a hallmark of infidelity. Secrets and lies and deceit. Men and women honest in other areas of life become expert liars in the midst of affairs. Dishonesty shatters the foundational trust of the marital relationship. Initially, a heavy fog covers the hope of rebuilding trust. The lies are too many, too personal, too eyeball-to-eyeball to believe trust is possible again.

All of affair recovery is really about rebuilding trust. Exploring our emotions, examining our story from the beginning, facing the mirror, lifting our doubts to God: all these are elements in the construction of rebuilding trust. Truly trust must be rebuilt. It was given once but now a tedious building project from chaos is required.

"How can I trust you again?" flashes as a daily question for the betrayed to ponder and the betrayer to honor. New construction would be much easier than this remodel from the rubble. Yet, the repurposing of the rubble yields a beauty not possible without it.

REBUILDING TRUST
IN CHAOS

BEN

With the revelation of the affair, trust (and my heart) shattered like a porcelain teacup. At times, gluing the scattered pieces into a strong vessel seemed impossible. After being lied to for three years, how could I possibly believe anything she said? I wanted to believe Ann, but words or actions would graze a wounded area of my soul stirring pain, fear and mistrust. I didn't know where to begin.

The only place to start rebuilding trust in an affair-strewn marriage is in the chaos.

I wanted formulas and guarantees that she would never cheat again. That's another way of saying that I never wanted to hurt so deeply again. But guarantees are for products not relationships. No explicit formula exists for rebuilding trust - only guidelines. The guidelines can lead to an overall movement in a positive direction. The movement in rebuilding trust typically resembles a lurching two-steps-forward, one-step-back process. Sometimes Ann and I danced a high speed cha-cha. One, two, chachacha. Step, step, forwardbackforward.

At first, I felt guilty for not trusting my own wife. I was relieved to learn that I wasn't required to *give* trust. Because of the multitude of lies and concealment, Ann needed to *earn* my trust. Earning or regaining trust requires a constant consideration of the offended person's feelings. Ann consistently checked in with me concerning the impact of her decisions on my heart. She told a new company that she wouldn't travel out of town when she learned new employees traveled to the home office for training. I wasn't up to her traveling alone at this point. She also declined an offer to share rides to work with a male coworker though they both drove 30 miles along the same road. Seemingly innocent time spent together creates a situation in which many affairs begin, so Ann honored my request to drive separately. Her consideration of my feelings conveyed that my soul truly mattered to her again, which helped to incrementally restore trust between us.

As I said, there are no guarantees trust will be rebuilt. This both frustrated and freed me. At first, thoughts of divorce seemed like a magical way out of pain. Thoughts of not having to deal with the hard task of restoring trust allured me. Discussing the harsh realities of a broken marriage with our counselor helped immensely. He helped us see that divorce is a painful creator of a new set of problems instead of a magic elixir to eliminate my pain. I had a choice to struggle through the pain of rebuilding trust or enter new and different pain by divorcing Ann. During the initial crisis period (post revelation) was no time for me to make a decision about whether to end my marriage or not. My emotions were all over the place. I'm glad I didn't listen to naive friends and instead found wise input from a counselor, my chaplain and mature friends. They guided me to successfully navigate the troubled waters in our marriage.

Though I wanted to be rid of crazy-making and mistrustful thoughts, I came to accept the gradual process of restoring trust. Like the gradual lengthening of days following the darkest day at the start of winter, perhaps the slow walk to restoring trust starts like the darkest day in northern Alaska. There was more darkness than light, but the percentage of light in our lives grew as we moved through the process. As much as I wanted to rush rebuilding trust, it took time.

It took time because our life was in chaos. Though difficult to see at first, there is hope in chaos. In *False Intimacy*, counselor Dr. Harry Schaumburg says, "More often than not, we define faith as seeing God in the circumstance. But in chaos we never see God. Faith should be defined as knowing that God sees us in the chaos."

God formed the universe out of chaos. Trusting in this helped me believe in His formational power in my marriage. He built a solid foundation in our relationship from the chaos. Rebuilding trust surfaced new levels of maturity in me. It required more heart and soul than I ever knew I had. Staying present in the chaos gave God a chance to create a beautiful relationship from the shattered pieces of our hearts.

What actions do you specifically need from your spouse to help restore trust?

KEEPING SECRETS
AND TELLING LIES

BEN AND ANN

Total honesty is a must. Total honesty is a must. Total honesty is a must.

Keeping secrets *intentionally* damages a relationship, so secrets need to be disclosed immediately. Other thoughts and memories may come as you move through the process. Share as those surface, and extend grace as they are offered. See it as a good thing (even though difficult) when more truth is brought into the light.

I {Ann} feared the consequences of telling Ben my secrets. I thought, "I don't want to tell him about that. It would hurt too much. I've already caused enough pain." Doesn't that sound noble? Not so much. It's just denial. The damage had already been done. Not telling the truth was all about me, the secret keeper. It was more about covering my ass than protecting his heart.

My mask was blown off in a moment when my affair was revealed. All the lies, cheating and sneaking came out in a powerful blast. It took courage I didn't know I had to tell Ben the truth that day. It was a process, but soon I was able to tell the truth more consistently. Being honest in this new way gave me courage the next time I faced the dilemma of keeping a secret or sharing truth. I fought through heaps of shame and soon told the truth even - no, especially - when it made me look bad. Becoming truthful and honest brought hope to our relationship.

I {Ben} was faced with the sky-high challenge of forgiving Ann's lies as she told me the truth. Forgiving lies is one of the harder aspects of rebuilding trust. We all deserve to know the truth about our own lives. I just wanted to know the truth about all that happened so I could make decisions based on truth. After three years of lies, I didn't know what was true about my life anymore. A bazillion questions constantly peppered my brain at warp speed. Were there other guys? What else has she lied about? Can she change? Does she want to change?

I watched her like Homer Simpson watches a McRib. I constantly listened for partial truths or whole lies. Ann made a commitment to total honesty; yet, lying had become such a habit that she did it when she didn't need to. One time, I heard Ann tell our daughter an inconsequential lie. I called her on it.

{Ben} "Why do you feel the need to lie?"

{Ann} *"I don't know."*

Well, "I don't know" didn't cut it any more. I needed her to figure out why she was lying and tell me the truth or we weren't going anywhere. Fortunately, she did the hard work of getting to the core issue and changed. Along the way, it was important for me to understand that her change in this area would be a process. This wasn't permission to keep lying. It was me understanding that lying had become an ingrained, involuntary response for her.

I {Ann} began to tell the truth to Ben about my whereabouts, my life and my heart. Some days were easier than others. It was hard, and it didn't always go well. When I found myself telling a lie, I learned to come clean as fast as possible because I discovered that the hardest truth is easier to deal with than the cheapest lie.

My intentional secrets had kept Ben at a distance. He couldn't know the real me with my secrets standing in the way. I learned that the real me is who he wanted all along. Giving him the real me restored trust.

"Have nothing to do with the fruitless deeds of darkness, but rather expose them. But everything exposed by the light becomes visible, for it is light that makes everything visible"

(EPHESIANS 5:11, 13-14).

Are there truths still concealed? Take the big step of bringing all into the light.

A DISTANT HOPE

BEN AND ANN

A primary requirement for rebuilding trust is time accountability. Ann was willing to be accountable for her time, which became a key element in learning to trust her again. At times she felt suffocated by it. However, it communicated to me her sincerity and understanding about the pain her affair caused. This adjustment also illustrated her value for our relationship. Her actions in her affair communicated the opposite. I felt rejected and minimized, so her willingness to share the minute logistics of her day reestablished my importance to her.

I {Ann} accounted for 1,440 minutes of the day, every day. Being accountable was incredibly challenging and frustrating. Some people thought that Ben was a controlling husband because he desired to know my whereabouts all the time. They didn't understand because they didn't know about the affair. I never felt Ben was controlling. I knew he needed this in order to trust me again. It soothed Ben's soul for me to stay accountable. Even being five minutes late was painful for him as triggers for the betrayed are easily activated. Five minutes could seem like an hour filled with trauma-fueled affair fears for Ben.

There were times I was weary of being accountable. I didn't want to call, dammit! But I chose to be obedient, as much or more to God than to Ben. I had a distant hope for what our marriage could truly be. I don't believe in fake-it-until-you-make-it. I believe in facing the truth head on, pain and all, and I chose to respond out of something deep within me that held a higher vision of what our marriage was intended to be.

Another important aspect of rebuilding trust is a consistent discussion about the general issues of marriage. Exploring the issues is more important than determining who is right or wrong. Remember this concept. It will serve you well - long past healing from the affair - because learning to have conflict in a constructive manner rather than determining a winner is essential.

We can't stress enough the value of discussing what healthy intimacy looks like with regards to feelings, physical touch, spirituality, and social activities. Every honest, open conversation (whatever the topic) enriches trust. Trust grows when both spouses humbly own their contributions to the problems in the marriage.

In what ways have you wounded each other throughout the relationship? Are there past disagreements that haven't been resolved? How do you hide your hearts from one another?

HOLLOW FORGIVENESS

BEN

So accountability and examining the marriage relational issues are of primary importance, but sometimes they are so difficult that a couple will interrupt their own progress. Oddly enough, apology and forgiveness can be the interrupting culprits.

Often, Christians feel compelled to forgive right away. We're supposed to forgive, right? Yet all the wounds from an affair take time to emerge; if forgiveness comes too early it can be hollow. That hollowness can inhibit us from discussing the ups and downs of the relationship since its inception. It took time to discover all the ways Ann wounded me. I felt angry when it dawned on me that we bought two houses over the three years she was in the affair. I didn't realize this until the year anniversary of purchasing the second home. If I had known would I have wanted to buy either home with her? No way. It was another wound to forgive. Knowing forgiveness is a process that occurs over time was freeing and helped me process all the feelings around the affair.

Some people are apologyholics. I'm sorry, I'm sorry, I'm sorry. Save it. I remember a time in counseling when Ann told the counselor she didn't know what to say when I shared my hurt with her. She usually just kept saying, "I'm sorry." After a while, apologies felt meaningless. Really all I needed from her in that moment was to listen. Just listen. She also learned an apology served to help her feel less guilty instead of being a real gift to me, the one she betrayed. She learned to ask what I was feeling concerning different matters then listen and keep her apology to herself. I felt validated and pursued by her presence and focus on my soul.

Do either of you struggle with apologizing too much? Rarely apologizing? What are your fears underneath these actions?

GOD REWARDS IN LOVE

BEN

*D*id we always want to be present with one another as we went through this process of rebuilding trust? Heck no, but we were obedient. Choosing obedience to God is part of accountability in the restoration process. Often we chose to live by obedience, letting God work at His pace. Sometimes His pace seems painfully slow to us. Really the slowness is more about the deep, penetrating nature of the betrayal, and He wants to be sure we take the time to go to those depths.

Life must be yielded to God in the midst of the pain. This doesn't mean you won't wrestle with God during this time. Our spirituality and relationship with God is clarified and deepened in dealing with betrayal. Is He really good? Is He really powerful? Sure doesn't feel like it at the moment. In my case, as I wrestled with those questions I also held in tension (holding in tension means holding two truths seemingly opposite that are both true) that He was the best thing (person/relationship) that ever happened to me.

What we did out of obedience, God rewarded in love. This is such a powerful truth. Those rewards may not be felt instantly, but they will come. You'll just have to borrow our hope on that one.

At times, when the steps are backward stumbles, it's easy to feel like giving up. But remember, God doesn't write "finished" on our foreheads when we screw up. Restoration requires more of you than you can imagine and feels like a lot of work, but He isn't done with you.

It also will require letting God work at His pace. We can experience Him as total molasses sometimes. In reality, we underestimate the depth of our souls, and we underestimate the time it takes for deep, inside-out transformation.

Rebuilding trust challenged us, humbled us and eventually rewarded us with a close, loving relationship.

How do you struggle with trusting God?

CHOW FUNS

BEN

As you rebuild trust, it is important to remember what drew you to your spouse. In the pain and chaos of an affair it is easy to recolor your history - to say we never really had much in common or never had much fun together. During one of our first counseling appointments the counselor asked us what was good about our relationship in the beginning. I couldn't think of anything. Our whole relationship seemed fake and dark through the coffee-colored glasses blurring my vision.

Fortunately, I recovered some clearer lenses to see our story. These rationalizations of not having any good in our relationship aided in minimizing pain instead of facing reality head on. For most couples, the truth is they really just enjoyed spending lots of time together in the beginning. Though it can be painful at first, try to remember what specifically brought joy early in your relationship.

The movie *The Story of Us* has a great scene to illustrate this. In the movie, Ben (Bruce Willis) and Katy (Michelle Pfeiffer) are married with two kids. Their marriage is in trouble, and divorce seems inevitable.

The kids are coming home from summer camp, and the couple decides they will tell them about the divorce after picking them up from the bus. They discuss going to Chow Funs restaurant for dinner but decide they can't talk there so they choose another place.

The night before, in the space of her solitude, Katy takes a long look at all the family pictures on the wall. Memories of their shared life together pour through her mind. The following day, she and Ben are on the way to meet the kids. Memories again speed through her brain from their dating years, engagement, wedding, kids being born, kids having crises like pets dying, Ben's dad dying, fights, hot sex, tender times, angry times, doors slamming, phones slamming, I love yous and I hate yous.

They arrive to gather the kids from the bus. As the kids get in the car, Katy stands away a bit and tells Ben, "I think we should go to Chow Funs."

Ben: "Chow Funs? I thought we both agreed we couldn't really talk at Chow Funs."

Katy: "I know."

Ben: "What are you saying?"

Katy: "I'm saying Chow Funs."

Ben: "Are you saying Chow Funs because you can't face telling the kids? Cause if that's why you are saying Chow Funs don't say Chow Funs."

Katy: "That's not why I'm saying Chow Funs. I'm saying Chow Funs because we're an us. There's a history here, and histories don't happen over night. You know in Mesopotamia or ancient Troy or somewhere back there, there are cities built on top of other cities, but I don't want to build another city. I like this city. I know where we keep the Bactine and what kind of mood you're in when you wake up by which eyebrow is higher; and you always know that I'm quiet in the morning and compensate accordingly. That's a dance you perfect over time. And it's hard. It's much harder than I thought it would be, but there's more good than bad, and you don't just give up. And it's not for the sake of the children, but God they're great kids. Aren't they? And we made them! There were no people there, and then there were people! And they grew. I won't be able to say to some stranger that Josh has your hands or remember how Erin threw up at the Lincoln Memorial. Then, I'll try to relax.

Let's face it. Anybody is going to have traits that get on your nerves. I mean why shouldn't it be your annoying traits? I'm no day at the beach, but I do have a good sense of direction so at least I can find the beach. Which is not a criticism of yours it's just a strength of mine. And God you're a good friend, and good friends are hard to find. Charlotte said that in *Charlotte's Web,* and I love the way you read that to Erin, and you take on the voice of Wilbur the Pig with such commitment even when you're bone tired. That speaks volumes about character, and ultimately isn't that what it comes down to - what a person is made of? Because that girl in the pith helmet is still in here. "Beeboo, beeboo." I didn't even know she existed until I met you. And I'm afraid if you leave I may never see her again. Even though I said at times you beat her out of me. Isn't that the paradox? Haven't we hit the essential paradox? Give and take, push and pull, yin and yang, the best of times, the worst of times. I think Dickens said it best, the Jack Spratt of it - he could eat no fat, his wife could eat no lean. But that doesn't really apply here does it? I guess what I'm trying to say here is I'm saying Chow Funs because I love you."

Ben: "I love you, too."

When hope waned, Ben and Katy developed a renewed commitment to their relationship as Katy revisited their shared story, the highlights and the lowlights. Spend some time really pondering your shared story. Spend time alone together. Make sure no distractions get in your way of connecting with each other on a deep level. That means no kids, no Facebook, no television, etc. No distractions give you the time and space to tell stories to one another about your dating years and pre-affair years of marriage. Don't let the present pain color it all. Fight to remember the good as well as the difficult.

What are your favorite/significant memories of your relationship?

HOW DID WE GET HERE?

On their wedding day, most couples can't imagine a time when an affair could invade their marriage. My guess is you didn't fathom that possibility. So what in the world happened to our happy dreams of love ever after? How did one (or both) of us become vulnerable to an affair?

From before birth, God, culture and parents shape our view of the world. As we grow much of this rests under the surface where we learn not to mention it, or perhaps in our busyness we simply don't notice. We live in denial with unhealthy statements like: "I'm just going to forget that ever happened," "Mom didn't really mean that," "Dad was drunk when he hit me so it wasn't really him," "All families keep secrets," "I'll just pretend to be confident," "Men aren't suppose to feel," "Crying is weak, women have to just keep going," "If I don't take care of myself nobody will," "I only feel alive when I have a sex."

Like the impact of our culture and parents rests under the surface, so does God's design for us as male and female. Most of us never really ponder with depth what it means to have a masculine or feminine soul.

The deepest we usually dive is to examine our roles in marriage. But masculinity and femininity involves much greater depths than our roles. What did God have in mind in making a he and a she? Perhaps you've heard a sermon on being male and female and left feeling invalidated or thinking you couldn't be yourself by that definition. In this section, we desire to validate you and your gender knowing that living connected to your design will enhance connection in your marriage.

SONS AND DAUGHTERS
OF GOD

BEN AND ANN

Our gender plays a significant role in relationships. Generally, men fail to speak and move by avoiding. We fear being destroyed by disrespect and failure. Women close off their hearts and are unwilling to risk pain and vulnerability through controlling tendencies. Avoidance and control are generally seen as the primary sin of men and women, respectively.

I {Ben} can see where I was weak as a man. There was no movement on my part toward Ann and no movement in life. I drowned my soul in alcohol; I had an emotional lover at work. I didn't know how to impact Ann's soul, so I quit trying.

I {Ann} was a controlling woman. I'd try to tell Ben how to drive, where to drive and when to turn (even though he is the one with the internal GPS, and I can't find my way out of a paper bag with a map). I constantly monitored him. I tried to be the all-American supermom - working, serving in five roles at church, leading Girl Scouts, baking for all the events and positioning myself in the Clean House Derby. I gave a lot but can see now that my motive was more about avoiding my own heart than blessing others.

I {Ben} began to wake up as a man following the affair. I began to pursue Ann with courage, yet strongly and tenderly. I began to see myself as a protector of my family. My primary identity began to transform to son of God. In turn I began to experience more respect from Ann. I began to realize she really did believe in me.

I {Ann} realized first and foremost I was a daughter of God. I began to see that trusting Ben wasn't the hard part. It was trusting God that I couldn't force myself to do. I felt as if we were on a stagecoach heading for a cliff and I had the reins in hand. I began to see the bigger problem wasn't an unwillingness to hand them to Ben, but an unwillingness to hand them to God. Through fear, with courage, the reins slipped from my hands to God's. I learned to rest. The juggernaut of activity slowed. In the stillness I experienced being cherished, and accepted that I didn't have to do it all.

You, too, are called to be a son or daughter of God. Embrace this calling on your soul, grow into it, and live fully and completely with this identity declared as your own.

Where have you avoided as a man or controlled as a woman?

FAMILY STUFF

BEN AND ANN

To grow into our masculinity and femininity we had to return to our families to understand how some misgivings about gender originated. Much of what we know about being men and women comes to us through our families. We both grew up in families with many good qualities, but as we like to say, every family has dysfunction. It's just the level of dysfunction that varies.

I {Ben} spent lots of time with my dad playing golf. It's a cool thing to compete and kick butt with your dad. My mom took good care of my brothers and me. On the other hand, there were negative themes.

I learned I could coast in other areas since I did well in sports. Golf was my identity. In high school, I won conference as a freshman and state as a junior and senior. I played for Mizzou in college earning All-Big-8 honors as a senior and playing on the Big-8 Championship team that ended Oklahoma State's 14-year victory run. The problem was that I believed my value came from my score. If I shot 68, I was a great guy. If I shot 86, I was a piece of crap.

Another theme I learned was drinking was necessary to have fun. I started getting drunk when I was 13. When I was 14, I went out with my brother on my birthday. I bought a case of beer with my birthday money for my brother and his friends; I ended up leaning out of the car throwing up. Why I thought this was fun and continued getting drunk is a great question. There was certainly a deep desire to be liked and also a desire to numb my heart and any wounds and insecurities.

The third theme was that it was okay to lie to women. I wasn't taught to honor my wife, to touch her soul, to cherish her. When I was about 13, I was at the mall with my dad. He made a call on the pay phone to a woman. (Remember, no cell phones back then.) When he hung up he turned to me and said, "Don't tell your mom about that call."

I relied on sports for my value, drank to have *fun*, and treated women as something to make me feel good - not as daughters of God, worthy of respect and honor.

My {Ann} dad and mom both worked hard. They had four kids in five years so we certainly kept them on their toes. I learned to be involved, how to enjoy scrumptious food from the garden and eat it heartily, and I inherited motivation to succeed from them. Yet as I look at my life, I see the theme of sexual sin stand out like a blinking neon sign in a pitch-black window. Three of the four kids conceived children out of wedlock, and two had affairs. One of my siblings had an affair that ended his marriage, married his affair partner and subsequently had another affair.

Performance became a way for me to feel valued and accepted. So I made sure my picture was on almost every page in the yearbook. I was involved in loads of activities at school but only if I thought I would be good at them. I didn't dare try something new that might make me look foolish if I couldn't do it well. Consequently, the wide variety of activities I participated in, I did well. I made good grades, played basketball, was the drum major for the marching band and had significant roles in plays. At school I was a model citizen.

Too bad that wasn't all that happened in my life during those years. Another theme for me was living a dual life. On the weekend I was a party girl and I often found myself in the back seat of someone's car. They usually wouldn't date me but I was good enough to be used sexually. The first time I had sex I didn't like it, but there was something about being wanted and desired that drew me. So like a dog going back to its vomit, I kept returning. The ability to live this dual life became a big factor leading to my affair after I was married.

Another theme I picked up from my family was conflict avoidance. From my perspective as their child, my parents avoided difficult conversations. I used to think it was a good thing that I only saw them fight once. Looking back, maybe they just swept stuff under the carpet. Ben and I started off doing the same thing. We avoided difficult conversations. We didn't deal with anything. Partly because we didn't know how. We had never been taught.

So our families possessed many good qualities but also many skewed assumptions on what it meant to be men and women. We both became tied up in what we did and not who we were.

Another factor for us comes in the form of birth order and both being the youngest. We grew up more accustomed to receiving rather than giving. We got our way more frequently than our older siblings. We've tried to redeem some of these traits as parents. We want our kids to know the importance of being wholly male and wholly female. Imperfectly for sure, I have tried to be a strong father for my daughter and son. I tried to enjoy my son versus instructing and evaluating him as he played football and rugby in high school. I also tried to be aware of my impact on my daughter though I failed terribly when in her early years of high school I labeled her participation in marching band as *mom's thing*. Even if I couldn't hear her instrument or see her marching it was still important for her to know I was present and that she mattered to me. I learned that after causing her some pain.

We had rites of passage for both children. For Payne's 13th birthday, men came over, ate a lot of meat, then each one gave Payne a gift and words initiating and inviting him into manhood. *For Stephanie's sixteenth birthday, I {Ann} shared meaningful gifts that tied into what it means to be a woman affirming the beauty that I see in Stephanie inside and out.* These have been rich times for the four of us. We have been blessed by intentionally speaking to our kids about gender. Our hope is our kids will continue to move into their design.

We know the journey of embracing your gender is a lifelong undertaking and a daily challenge. Looking at your family of origin is no day in the park either. Be encouraged, the journey is worthwhile to redeem the negative themes and emerge with a clearer vision of what it means to be wholly male and wholly female, to be a son and daughter of God.

As you look at the family you grew up in, what positive and negative themes emerge for you?

KING'S SPEECH THERAPY

BEN

If you're like me sometimes you skip over the questions. You'll miss out if you do that on next two reflections. These reflections will help you process your family of origin. We've included multiple questions to guide you. We encourage you to reflect and write on all that was good and bad in your life growing up. Talk about your memories with a close friend or counselor and ultimately with your spouse.

Like we said, taking stock of *your entire story*, from birth to the present, will bring growth and healing individually and with your spouse. *The King's Speech* is a movie that offers lessons in dealing with anger and soul trauma from our childhoods.

The movie's main character is Bertie (Colin Firth), the Duke of York, who later becomes King Edward VI. Bertie stutters and stammers especially when nervous. The movie opens as Bertie addresses a large crowd at Wembley Stadium, which is also being broadcast on new technology - the radio. Awkward pain fills the crowd as they watch and hear him utter a syllable or word every few seconds. I feel a similar cringe inside me when ESPN replays a painful injury over and over.

One evening Bertie shares insight (foreshadowing) into the truth of his story as he goes from a shame filled stammerer to the courageous leader of the English people during World War II. He tells his daughters a tale of a young prince whose mother turned him into a penguin and sent him to be with the other penguins with wings but unable to fly. The penguin eventually makes a miraculous swim, moving up the Thames and into Buckingham Palace where he turns into an albatross with giant wings capable of scooping up both his daughters (he playfully hugs Margaret and Elizabeth), giving and receiving an abundance of love.

Eventually, Bertie talks with an unconventional therapist, Lionel Logue (Geoffrey Rush). Lionel doesn't want to just teach technique. He wants to know more about Bertie's life, heart and inner world. But Bertie doesn't want to talk about his family.

Not talking about the family is a hallmark of a dysfunctional family. Post affair Ann and I took deep looks into our family history. It was an essential part of our healing.

Lionel moves into technique first to help gain Bertie's trust. Among prescribed activities Bertie is to rock back and forth, from left foot to right foot, while swinging his arms and saying nursery rhymes. The rocking back and forth or dancing the waltz brought movement and continuous flow to Bertie as he dealt with his stammering. The waltz is interesting in this manner because it is a three-step dance that alternates the initial foot. Left right left then right left right. Left and then right. The rocking is reminiscent of modern day EMDR trauma therapy (Eye Movement

Desensitization and Reprocessing) that was initially used to treat combat veterans with Post-Traumatic Stress Disorder or PTSD. Lionel's background was with battle-worn PTSD victims.

I've begun utilizing EMDR in my practice for trauma recovery including the trauma for the betrayed and betrayer that comes from the revelation of an affair.

Gradually Bertie opens up about the lack of closeness with his father, King George V. Bertie learned to live a life of fear from his father. His father said, "I was afraid of my father, and my children damn well are gonna be afraid of me." As WWII approaches, the king discusses Bertie's eventual succession to the throne. He mentions the family. Bertie responds, "We're not a family, we're a firm."

The king turns ill and knows he heads towards death. He says to Bertie, "Who will stand between us, the jackboots and the proletarian abyss? You?" A knife thrust straight to the heart of a son who desires his father's belief in his courage. A turning point comes when King George V dies. Bertie tells Lionel about his dad's last words, "Bertie has more guts than the rest of his brothers put together." Bertie adds, "But he couldn't say that to my face!" Bertie longs for his father's affirmation.

We'll continue with Bertie's story in the next reflection. For now, find a quiet space to ponder the following questions:

Was fear a tactic in your home? How has fear hindered your marriage?

What wounds have you received from your father and mother? Others?

Are there words you longed to receive from your father and mother? What are they?

Where do you hope to find giant wings of strength and freedom like Bertie? What changes does this mean for you and your life?

KING'S SPEECH THERAPY II

BEN

_B_ertie learned he was defective in many ways. He was naturally left-handed, but was punished as a boy if he used his left hand. So he used his right. Lionel pointed out that many stammerers are natural left-handers who weren't allowed to be themselves. Another message of defectiveness came when Bertie's brothers teased him, "Bbbbbbbbbertie." They mocked him and were encouraged in this shaming by their father. Bertie's high sense of shame was captured in a brief exchange where Lionel responds to a compliment from Bertie by saying, "What are friends for?" Bertie says, "I wouldn't know."

Bertie's first nanny was cruel. She loved his older brother, David, more. She would pinch Bertie slyly just before passing him to his mother. He began crying, and mom passed him back. Then the nanny wouldn't feed him, which developed life-long stomach problems for Bertie. His parents didn't notice her trick for three years. The pinching and withholding food were forms of abuse.

In addition to dancing the waltz, play and cussing undergird Bertie's healing. After his father's death,

Bertie feels free to play. He becomes more vulnerable with his heart and story. He assembles a model airplane, an activity he was never allowed to pursue as a child. Play is a break from busyness and helps him regain a sense of innocence. Play becomes an important piece of healing.

Bertie leaves therapy after a conflict with Lionel. Yet after David taunts him once again with "Bbbbbbbertie" leaving Bertie speechless, Bertie returns to therapy and cusses as he shares the story of the taunting. Lionel says, "Vulgar but fluent. You don't stammer when you swear."

Bertie meekly says another cuss word to which Lionel retorts, "Is that the best you can do?"

"Bloody bugger to you beastly bastard. Shit shit shit shit shit shit shit shit shit shit shit shit shit." Lionel then asks, "Do you know the *f* word?" Bertie responds with a long string of *f* words and buggitys and other words as he moves around the room.

Some may say this language is bad because it violates Ephesians 4:29, "Watch the way you talk. Let nothing foul or dirty come out of your mouth. Say only what helps, each word a gift." In normal situations I don't enjoy hearing folks constantly using the *f* word.

Yet, this wasn't a normal situation. Evil was sweeping the continent due to Hitler. A man who was going to be the voice of the free world in Europe stood handcuffed by shame. Fear manifested in the form of stuttering effectively silenced his courage. Bertie's cuss words represented the spitting out of venom from the attempts of the evil one to take him out instead of delivering brave and energizing speeches during the Second World War.

As Hitler stalked Europe, I believe the evil one stalks marriages today. A few coarse words in private are miniscule compared to the significant cost and devastation to a family due to an unnecessary divorce. This may sound a bit dramatic, but the pain I see in those going through divorce following an affair is dramatic. Fortunately, Bertie continued healing as we hope you can.

"Shit shit shit shit shit shit shit shit shit shit shit shit." (No, no, no evil nanny, I will not be held down in fear.) "Buggity, buggity, buggity." (God's grace is bigger than any shame my brothers and my father heaped on me with their relentless pokes and prods.) "Fuck, fuck, fuck, fuck." (Evil one you will not silence me as I speak for Britain as the German church bows down to der Fuhrer. Fuck der Fuhrer! I HAVE A VOICE!)

Bertie finally finds freedom. I think Lionel's therapy is brilliant and could be helpful in expressing the anger that comes from the trauma of an affair or previous trauma. Find a private place, move about, maybe waltz a little and spit out some venom from your wounds.

Where can you recapture a sense of play in your life?

In what ways did your family communicate to you that you were defective? How does that impact you today?

Has there been emotional, physical or sexual abuse in your past? Find a close friend or counselor to help process this aspect of your story. It is essential to grant yourself time and space to explore the impact this abuse had on you.

Reflecting on both of the King's Speech reflections, what are the major positive and negative themes from your family of origin? Be prepared for this to take time and energy and may take weeks and months to unpack. All of our families of origin are a complicated mix of beauty and disaster.

IS SEX THE ULTIMATE ANSWER?

BEN AND ANN

*I*n addition to our families, our culture impacts our views on gender as well. Frequently, this impact is negative.

Our culture asks us often to be sexual beings at the cost of our true selves. In other words, sex is pitched as the ultimate answer to solving the problems in our lives without thought to the cost we pay with our souls.

{Ann} Women are told we are unlovely if we don't have supermodel looks.

My experience as a counselor has taught me that women with striking looks struggle just as deeply internally because others assume that since they look good they don't have any real relational or life issues. In other words, their pain isn't taken seriously resulting in even deeper wounds.

God has much more to say on the issue of beauty, internal and external. It's not true, you know, the old saying, "sticks and stones can break my bones but words can never hurt me." After years of believing lies, I finally learned to listen to His voice over all the others that used to scream at and shred my soul with awful, hurtful words.

{Ben} Men are told we don't have what it takes unless we are scoring on the field, in the financial world or in bed.

Pornography is a lure that gives us the sense of being a man without requiring any risk. But it always takes more than it gives, ultimately thinning our souls and making deeper relationship more difficult. We're left feeling even more lonely and isolated.

Our transient culture challenges lasting relationships, an issue for both men and women. We need friends to grow with and remind us of God's involvement in our lives.

A significant piece of healing from Ann's affair occurred when I attended a weekly, early morning meeting with a group of men. Being authentic with them gave me permission to grieve the losses from the affair on a deeper level. The masculine validation of my wounds and tears built strength, not weakness, in my soul.

What cultural expectations have impacted how you live as male or female?

LIVING THE SMALL DAILY DECISIONS

BEN

Men are designed to protect in strength and tenderness. This doesn't mean women are incapable of taking care of themselves. It does mean that men are meant to have an eye on the deep value of a woman as a daughter of God "and to present her to himself as a radiant church, without stain or wrinkle or any other blemish, but holy and blameless" (Ephesians 5:27 NIV).

The opposite of this scenario is a domestic abuse situation where a man diminishes a woman psychologically and physically. Instead of a woman feeling safe and valued she'll live in fear of a man and detest herself due to his belittling.

As men, we are called to die daily to our self-centered desires out of love for our wives. Most men will commit to jumping in front of a truck if it is headed for his wife. Sure, what are the odds of that happening? The real call to die to self is on a daily basis. Will I give up watching golf on TV to help my wife get ready for the party she is hosting? Will I watch her favorite show with her instead of taking in all of Sunday night football? Will I go out to eat Chinese with her when my favorite is Mexican?

These are small examples, but loving your wife is communicated in a ton of seemingly small decisions each and every moment. These other-centered decisions grow hearts more open to love. If decisions are constantly self-centered, love evaporates.

Grace is necessary as we live out this calling imperfectly. We're all going to blow it. Sometimes we blow it in little ways and sometimes in big ways. If grace flows both ways between a husband and wife odds increase for a close marriage.

Men, when we mess up it is important to not cover ourselves in shame and then isolate. I know I'm tempted to hole up in the man cave bathing in my shame. Hiding communicates to our wives that we don't love them - or more personally that she isn't loveable. All she'll know is that you don't want to be beside her. So when you blow it know that God's grace does indeed flow your way. Let it carry you through your shame to move towards your wife in tender strength.

What small daily decisions can you make to bless your wife? What small decisions by your husband would communicate love to you?

CRAVE CONNECTION

ANN

When God uttered the words, "It is not good for man to be alone" in Genesis 2, I believe He was in essence saying, "He needs more." He realized man had relational needs beyond what He could offer. Adam needed someone he could talk with face to face; he needed someone he could touch; he needed someone with skin on.

Immediately following this realization, God tried finding that someone amongst the animals and birds He created, but none were suitable. So God, in all His brilliance, created woman. He created us to fill that relational need. Our primary purpose of creation was to relate to man, really to anyone within our world. Our primary function is to be relational. So what do we do with that?

Well, I know what I've done with it. I've run from it. I've hidden from it. I've tried to control my way out of it. I feared my heart and what it would say about me. I feared getting too close, or should I say I feared others getting too close to me. I kept others at a distance with a know-it-all attitude, used more words than anyone needs to use or that anyone wants to hear, controlled every conversation into a self-centered monologue of my own stories that had very little substance. Even though my soul was created to crave connection, my heart and mind didn't know how to connect with others.

After the revelation of my affair, I became determined to learn what it meant to be relational. I learned it had more to do with authenticity and connection than with what I thought I knew and feared. As you venture into this scary realm of authentically connecting with your heart, remember that you were created for this. Your mind may not understand what that means, but your heart and soul can grow into the woman God designed you to be rather than the woman the world has demanded you be.

And guys, women want to know that you want to *try* to understand us, even though sometimes *we* don't understand us. This should come in the form of knee-to-knee, face-to-face conversation. We know that shoulder-to-shoulder is generally more comfortable for you, but remember Ephesians 5 that says a husband's love is marked by giving, not getting? Yeah, that's the kind of listening I'm talking about. We want your full attention. We don't want you to watch the game with one eye and gaze lovingly into our eyes with the other.

If it's the game you've been waiting all week to watch, let us know you'll give us your full attention as soon as the game is over. We would rather you put down the book you are reading and focus your attention on *our* words than someone else's. And if you connect more deeply with your 923 friends on Facebook than with your wife (this applies to us, too, ladies), a shift in priorities may be in order.

And please just listen to us. Don't try to fix, just listen. If we need a solution to a problem, we promise to be clear on that. When you don't listen to us, as wrong as it might be, the temptation is to find someone else to share the deepest part of our hearts with as we try to figure out this *created-to-be-relational* part of our souls. Sometimes this can be healthy in the form of loving friendships with other women who will hold us accountable for our actions and words and who will hold us up to the One who listens to us all. Sometimes this can be disastrous (and perhaps the reason you're reading this book) in the form of an all-too-friendly acquaintance who would jump at the chance to show just how good a listener he can be. This is when we enter the danger zone. Know why? Because we were designed to crave connection. We were built for it. And sometimes we let that craving cloud our judgment, just like it does when we get a craving for a big slice of chocolate cake for breakfast. Be our chocolate cake so we aren't tempted by that big slice of danger that *will* drive a wedge between us with disastrous consequences.

Ladies, how have you embraced or shunned the relational side of your design as a woman?

Men, how have you embraced or shunned the relational side of your wife's design as a woman?

LOVE, TENDERNESS
AND A BIT OF EXCITEMENT

ANN

So women are created to be relational. But wait, that's not all! As women, we are also designed to invite. Our bodies are physically designed to invite, but we are also designed to invite relationally.

Let's look at the physical invitation. God was intentional as He created man and woman that their bodies would fit together perfectly, in perfect union, coming together into something beautiful and soul bonding. Our world has done much to skew our vision of this beautiful bond and make it something less than it is. Our world has also done much to discourage a woman from inviting her man to be with her. This includes our shame from past experiences such as abuse and promiscuity, comparison to images real and imagined that fill a man's mind, inadequacy felt from discouraging words shared during intimate moments and inadequacy felt from never learning what it means to truly invite.

Do any of these describe you? They have all described me at some moment in time. What I am learning is that shame, comparison and inadequacy are nothing compared to the richness of an invitation that is met with love, tenderness and, yes, a bit of excitement.

Now let's look at the relational invitation. As scary as it is to invite our man physically, I imagine most women have as much (or more) fear bound up in inviting a man into their souls. Inviting him into our soul requires a softness and tenderness that relinquishes control of the grip we have on the door to our heart. Admittedly, sometimes I can relax, let go and do this well; and yet there are also times when I slam the door, lock it tight and seemingly throw away the key. During these times I have come to understand the importance of inviting Ben in, not giving up on him or me.

He has at times been the cause of the slamming door, but at other times he has been a casualty of life. Fear presses in on me and causes me to isolate and close off everyone, including the man most dear to my soul. Remember what I said about women being created to be relational? Yup. That's why it is so important that we peer through the peephole of our shut-tight door. Open it, and usher in those most dear.

How does shame, comparison, inadequacy or fear stand in the way of inviting your husband physically or relationally? How would you like to be able to invite him towards you in the future?

WHAT'S YOUR QUESTION?

BEN AND ANN

At the end of Genesis 2, Adam was *really* excited to see Eve and they were naked and had no shame. They enjoyed close, open and intimate relationship with one another and especially with God. Circumstances quickly changed in Genesis 3. The serpent enticed them to eat from the Tree of Knowledge of Good and Evil and once they took those forbidden bites they realized they were naked and covered themselves. Take note that with their fig leaves they covered their areas of great difference and great intimacy. Thus began the long history of men and women covering and hiding themselves both physically and relationally.

This is typically referred to as The Fall in Christian circles, but I recently heard it referred to as The Turn by the author of Surfing for God, Michael Cusick. This is a more accurate description because Adam and Eve turned from God (making themselves vulnerable to the enticement of the serpent) rather than remaining in face-to-face relationship with Him.

Given that we all have a tendency to turn, let's ponder what our original design was and how we primarily turn from that design.

{Ben} Originally a man is designed to speak and move; yet since The Fall, or The Turn, his biggest sin is one of avoidance. At first, he splashed a little water on the garden and everything grew full. Easy. Post-Turn, the world began to produce thorns and thistles, challenging the initial ease of cultivation and growth. This applies not only to the black earth, but also to the verdant soil of man's soul. Man is still called to garden but growth won't always go according to plan. Cuts, bruises and exasperation are now a part of life. To avoid pain and failure, avoidance emerged as an easy way out. Man now wasn't sure of his strength in encountering the world. He turned and turns still. He questioned his ability to engage his world and began to cover his strength and avoid instead.

Man's biggest question then is do I have what it takes? Am I enough?

{Ann} Originally, a woman is designed to be relational, nurturing and inviting; yet since The Turn her biggest sin is one of control. Life in the garden was tranquil and filled with beauty. Her beauty glowed like the good light God created. She and man stood face-to-face with no masks and no walls. Woman never worried about rejection so her body and her heart were completely open, vulnerable and available to her man, to her world. Woman's days were fully safe until The Turn, when her whole world was turned upside down and became anything but safe. She then began to fear the cost to her heart and soul of being hurt and deceived in her vulnerability. She turned and turns still. She began to cover her beauty and control instead.

Woman's biggest question then, in light of the risk of rejection she fears, is do you think I'm beautiful (inside and out)? Do you see the light in me?

{Ben} Within the above categories there are many peculiarities, nuances and wonderful individual works of art created by God. So before we go on we want to address the fact that we are painting with very broad strokes. Ann has many great leadership qualities. She's a different type of leader and a better one than me in some ways. On the flip side I have a strong nurturing side. I can be tender and supportive. We're not talking about roles we *should* assume but about the deeper truth of God's design in our souls.

Again, because of The Turn, we now have these core questions. Let's explore them a little more as to what it looks like to ask that question deep in our masculine and feminine souls. Let's also look at how our primary sins as men and women disrupt the process of living out of the truth of God's design and lead us to instead live out of fear that our question won't be answered with a yes.

The man's question, "Do I have what it takes?", revolves around respect. A man desires *unconditional* respect. Shouldn't a man have to earn respect from his wife? Not necessarily. In the core of my soul I want to know that Ann believes I have what it takes even if I fail or freeze. I want her to see deeper into me with a vision for the good that exists within regardless of whether I acted in a way that earns respect in that moment.

Remember: the primary sin for women is control. Can you guess how men interpret this? Men interpret control as disrespect or a lack of belief in him. In other words, he feels contempt from her.

In the dating phase, men can actually like all the caretaking that comes with control. For example, I liked when Ann stepped up and did a lot which meant less was required of me. She made life easier (enabling my avoidance) for me. I didn't know it was also easier (encouraging her control) for her. I couldn't have put words to it then, but right from the start we were dealing with the control/avoidance dance.

{Ann} With a woman's question of "Do you think I'm beautiful inside and out?" comes our core desire for love – unconditional love. A woman wants to know that a man still cherishes and believes in the beauty of her heart even when she shows the unlovely side of her soul. I know that I am not lovely when I take over and take control, but I want to know that Ben will stay present with me when I'm like that, when I'm not at my best. When I am at my worst, Ben describes me as a whirring, spinning Tasmanian devil. Even then I want to know that he'll stay with me not avoid me. Even when my whirring and spinning self scratches and cuts him deeply, I want to know that he'll stay close and not disappear.

This is important because the primary sin for men of avoiding is interpreted by women as being unloved or unlovable. In other words, we feel wounded by the man when he essentially disappears.

Be sure and catch these next statements. When a man reacts out of sinful avoidance the answer his woman receives to her question (*Do you think I'm beautiful?*) is an emphatic NO. When a woman reacts out of sinful control the answer her man receives to his question (*Do I have what it takes?*) is an equally emphatic NO.

In other words, The Turn rigged the world to expose our sin. Our choice to counteract The Turn comes in the form of courage to look deeper into both our sin *and* our original design.

Be specific, what do you believe it means to love and respect your spouse? When have you felt your spouse believed in you? What ways do you desire your spouse to show you love and respect?

What do you believe it means to be cherished? When have you felt cherished by your spouse? What ways do you desire your spouse to cherish you?

NO STOMPING ALLOWED

BEN AND ANN

Considering the sensitivity of man's biggest question (do I have what it takes or am I enough?) and woman's biggest question (do you think I'm beautiful or do you see the light in me?) then an essential ingredient of a good marriage is learning not to stomp on your spouse's question! But as we said the world is rigged so that we stomp on each other's question and don't always know it.

As we mentioned earlier, Ann stomped on my question by telling me how to drive. I wasn't drive fast and dangerous. Her desire to be in control yielded comments about our exit coming up or instructing me that I wasn't going the best (in her eyes) way. I felt disrespected and sometimes wondered how I got anywhere without her in the car. *Ben stomped on my question by playing golf all day and going out and playing trivia with his buddies all night. Having been home alone all day with our young daughter, I was ready for some fun, but Ben didn't bother to ask me to go along for the good times. In his absence, a form of avoidance, I felt neglected and unloved.*

When our question is stomped on by our spouse we feel it. Our response might be a deep-sinking feeling, tears or anger. Often we aren't aware of exactly why we feel so strongly, we just know our heart has been missed big time. When this happens it's important to lean into the Gospel, lean into God and avoid attacking or checking out.

As counselor and author Dr. Emerson Eggerichs says in *Love and Respect*, men must have the courage to say something like "I'm feeling disrespected; have I been unloving?" Women have to summon their bravery and similarly offer: "I'm feeling unloved; have I been disrespectful?" The struggle is humbling yourself authentically by making one of these two brief statements and then engaging in an honest discussion.

{Ben} This is so challenging. My first impulse is rarely to humble myself. My first temptation when I feel disrespected is to lash out from my perceived wound. My second is to clam up and get out. It takes me a little bit to get down to what is most true in my soul and relate to Ann. I do want to love her and bless her.

{Ann} The same holds true for me. When I feel missed or unloved, I typically start hearing the whir of my internal gears grind to a halt. I begin to shut down and control what I can, which usually involves grabbing a broom, mop or sponge and cleaning the heck out of my house even if it doesn't need it. Like Ben, it takes me a little while to get to what is most true in my soul and put down that broom and take hold of his hand and heart.

For when we live out of our true design with a deeper dependence on Christ and act in an other-centered manner in our love for one another, our spouse will experience his or her questio stomped on but answered with a resoun(

When a man speaks and moves instea(a woman feels loved.

When a woman nurtures and invites instead of controlling a man feels respected.

Curiosity is an important element in knowing your spouse. Be curious about how the soul of your mate works in order to connect with them. Be an explorer of your spouse's soul. It's a scary, thrilling, rewarding adventure.

How have you stomped on your spouse's question? How can you be more curious about your spouse's soul?

CAN WE EVER BE CLOSE AGAIN?

ANN

When I speak about intimacy many merely hear a euphemism for sex. But intimacy is much more. Intimacy includes sex - praise Jesus, but intimacy also encompasses non-sexual touch, spiritual closeness, recreational togetherness, and emotional connection.

What can be so darn difficult about closeness in these areas?

Much of the difficulty stems from interacting with fallen people in a fallen world. In close relationships everyone receive wounds. In this, we learn that closeness can be dangerous so we become guarded to be safe. In extreme cases of abusive or addictive homes, we learn to be hyper alert in our guard duty. In not-so extreme cases, intimacy might not have been modeled or offered at home. Because it feels unfamiliar and unsafe, we learned to guard against it.

Guardedness, then, gets in the way of intimacy.

Now, you have two people in a relationship with intimacy issues also dealing with an affair. Wondering if you will ever be close again is a natural response to the betrayal. But find grace in this: many of us never learned how to truly be close to another in the first place, regardless of our upbringing. We just don't know how. Even if we do know some of what it means to be close, there is always more to learn. With humility, real intimacy is possible in all aspects of soul and senses.

MORE THAN JUST ONE TYPE

BEN

When we speak of intimacy, some think we are speaking only of sex. Wrong. Five different types of intimacy need to be developed by couples. The trick is to develop them all at about the same rate at about the same time. This is tricky because most of us default to one or two types of intimacy rather than put in the work to develop them all. It's also tricky because no one type of intimacy is more important than the other. They are just different, and each offer important qualities to our relationship. The five types of intimacy are: sexual, recreational, emotional, spiritual and non-sexual physical.

When we default to one type of intimacy, we stunt not only the growth of other types of intimacy, we also stunt the growth of our relationship. This was the case for us as our relationship became sexual within a month of our first date in college. As our relationship progressed and when tension developed we defaulted to sexual intimacy. "Let's not fight. Let's go to the bedroom and be close." This set the stage for a lot of trouble down the road because we were rarely intentional about developing emotional and non-sexual physical intimacy. We could be close skin-to-skin but not heart-to-heart.

In the beginning, we also had decent recreational intimacy because Ann is a pretty good basketball player. Her hoops skills were sexy to me. She was an all-district player in basketball-rich southeast Missouri. I could more easily relate to the jock Ann but had a tougher time connecting with the elegant Ann. While recreational intimacy is vitally important to men, it causes problems when it becomes a default at the expense of other types of intimacy. The relationship becomes all fun and no substance. One develops a superb ability to find fun activities to do but have difficulty finding the other's soul.

Ann admits she had a tougher time being in touch with her more tender side, too. This contributed to our difficulty developing emotional intimacy. You could say we were as emotionally connected as two immature college students could be. We could hang out all day and just enjoy each other's company, but we couldn't talk about the depths of our souls. Our hopes, dreams and desires went unshared and unnoticed by the person we were supposed to be the most connected to. Our emotional connection was flimsy at best and required much strengthening post-affair through an abundance of talking.

Our spiritual intimacy was nonexistent in the beginning because I wasn't a believer. Ann cringed when I slammed the door in the face of any evangelist that came knocking. Ann was a believer as a child but had tucked her beliefs away. Even once I became a believer and Ann renewed her commitment to Christ, we stumbled in this area. I would say this is one of the most difficult types of intimacy to truly develop because our spirituality accesses the deepest recesses of our hearts and souls. Our relationship with God is the most intimate relationship we have. And because we can't hide anything from Him, when we share our spirituality, it's as though we can't hide anything from each other either.

Since our default intimacy was sexual, non-sexual physical intimacy was something we intentionally developed post-affair. A caress on the cheek, snuggling on the couch, holding hands while walking all had to become habit rather than a passing thought. Ann needed to know that I wanted her for more than sex, that embracing her did not signify an intention of hopping in the sack.

Most couples, like us, default towards one or two types of intimacy early in their relationship. Your story has a lot to do with which are strong and which require growth.

Explore your story with respect to intimacy and uncover where your hearts, souls and bodies need connection.

CLUMSY AND MESSY

ANN

*B*efore my affair, we had a taste of true intimacy. While Ben was away several months for Army Reserve Basic Training we grew close through letters. Ben shared his inner world with me. I was able to receive that intimacy but was only minimally able to return it leading to an inability to sustain emotional intimacy upon his return.

In addition to not handling conflict well, we reverted to an old pattern of relying primarily on sexual intimacy. We still didn't know how to talk through tense situations, so we'd have make-up sex and move on without dealing with the issue. Never a good idea.

In order to break those old patterns, we looked at our story - all the way back to the beginning. Why go so far back, you say? Because it all matters. It's all important. Think of how the Bible starts. What are the first words on that first page? "In the beginning..." God doesn't start His story with Jesus and the glorious redemption of the cross. He starts with "In the beginning" and walks us through the mess of a story called the Old Testament before we get to the Grace of the New.

Our story didn't just start the day my affair was revealed, and it also didn't just start on our wedding day. Ben says he knows I was messed up when we started dating because I was dating him. We now know we were *both* a mess. The early years of our relationship and marriage were hard. Friends asked why I didn't divorce Ben. He drank a lot and didn't keep a steady job. I like to think Grace was at work even though we didn't know it at the time. Even so, we merely existed in the same house.

Post affair I told Ben how hard the early years were for me. I first had to admit to myself that I didn't feel cherished, that I felt used, that I resented the alcohol, that I felt more like his mom than his wife. Then came the hard part; speaking those words to him which took a lot of courage on both our parts, but he was able to hear my pain and own the ways he had hurt me from the beginning. On a broad scale, much broader than just the affair, we learned to own our pain and to give and receive grace.

One aspect of giving grace was learning to laugh at our idiosyncrasies. I can be clumsy. I break glasses and plates like a Russian who's had too much vodka. Only not on purpose. And without the vodka. Really. And Ben's dresser top and office desk often look like he just dumped a couple drawers on them. Yet, he still manages to find what he's looking for.

These quirks, and many others, used to cause great discord between us. We each wanted the other to be perfect and in many ways to be God. If that were possible, we would have had the ability to take away our insecurities, fears, shame and so much more. That was pressure placed on our relationship that neither of us could live up to. Neither one of us could touch the core of the other's soul that only God can touch to soothe it into safe, secure Love. Now, instead of demanding God-like perfection we accept and enjoy the peculiar parts of who we are. They make us unique, flawed and imperfect. Who wants to be perfect anyway?

What wounds remain unspoken and unheard from your early years? What idiosyncrasies drive you crazy and endear your spouse to you?

THE CORROSIVE ELEMENTS OF PAST ABUSE

ANN

While in graduate school for a counseling degree, I wrote a paper on sexual abuse. I pointed to clinical data and used other women's stories of abuse as examples of why sexual abuse is so damaging to the soul. Not once did it occur to me while writing that paper that what I had always referred to as an occurrence of being sexually used was in fact sexual abuse. Months later, while writing yet another paper, all the sexual sin in and around my life came crashing down around me. I was faced with the reasons I hid my heart, reasons I didn't trust, reasons I was unable to accurately describe the swirl of emotions in my soul. And so it goes for those of us who have been abused.

That abuse can be physical, emotional, verbal or sexual. Through the experience of being abused, we learn that being close is not safe, loving someone is not safe, and certainly letting another love us is not safe. Out of that inability to feel safe, abuse can cause intimacy to be terribly difficult.

Not only do we feel unsafe, we have trust issues. The ones we were supposed to trust – the people who were supposed to care for us and have authority over us, the ones who are supposed to love us the most – are more often than we like to admit the ones who abuse: fathers, stepfathers, mothers, stepmothers, coaches, even pastors. This atrocious breach of trust leads to an inability to trust most anyone. If those who are supposed to love us are the same ones that hurt us and cause so much pain to our hearts and souls, why would we ever trust another with either our hearts or our souls? What's more, we also lose our ability to trust ourselves, which consequently leads to an inability to trust our emotions.

Since we can't trust our feelings anyway, we shut off our emotions to avoid the pain of the abuse. This only works for so long. Then along comes someone that we want to be intimate with and we realize we don't know how. We have no clue how to truly experience the whole spectrum of emotion because we have limited our range of emotion in order to protect ourselves. Don't be surprised if we answer, "I don't know" if you ask us what we're feeling; most of the time, this is an honest answer. As part of this package of denying that we have emotions, we don't know how to love. Oh, some of us can put on a pretty good show. We can love you from the surface, but we can't love you from the depths of our being, and the shutdown is rarely just emotional. Many of us also shut down physically as well. We say, "My body betrayed me when I was abused by responding, and I won't allow it to betray me again."

We hide our true selves out of the shame of what has happened to us. We often feel the abuse was our fault. We fear if anyone discovered the truth of who we are and the ugliness of our story they will reject us, proving that we are unworthy of the love we crave deep down inside. Shame keeps us bound in the secrecy and isolation of the abuse. Shame keeps us from having hope that life will be any different. Shame keeps us from ever knowing love in its purest form.

You don't have to stay stuck in the nightmare of distrust and fear and shame. There is hope. Truly there is.

Have you received any abusive wounds? Maybe, like Ann, you've never named them. Find a trusted friend or counselor and tell your story to begin healing in this area.

HEALING PAST ABUSE

ANN

Healing past abuse is possible, but it is most certainly a process. Healing doesn't happen overnight for an abuse survivor - regardless of the type of abuse. Remember, all abuse gets in the way of intimacy, not just sexual abuse.

Much work is necessary for the abuse survivor, which can take place in the form of individual counseling, group counseling and a variety of individual processes. Individual counseling is beneficial because it keeps us in the process. We don't typically want to go through the pain of remembering, but knowing that we have someone – a caring counselor – who is for us and who is with us, helps us stay in the process.

We also highly recommend group work since one of the key components of abuse is the tendency for the abuser to isolate the abused so that they feel they are the only one. Let me assure you, you are not alone. Healing in a group setting highlights this truth spectacularly when you hear the stories of others and see and hear similarities with your own story in this safe environment. I can't begin to count the number of times I've heard women say, "I thought

I was the only one that happened to...." When this connection with another human being begins to happen, we begin to feel, really feel. We then gain the courage to face the shame and false belief that the abuse was our fault.

Truth is a key element of healing past abuse. Knowing the truth of your story shouts a powerful answer to the shame of abuse. The abuse is not your fault, was not your fault. You have been broken, but you can also be redeemed and restored. Experiencing healing through counseling and some intense personal work is amazing. You were created to love and be loved. That process may have been short circuited, but the longing is still there. Healing can bring the freedom to fulfill that longing.

The process isn't easy, but I can assure you it is *totally worth it*. It is worth being able to know you are cherished by your husband just because you're you. It is worth being able to sorrow with a friend over her impending divorce and all the realities that come with divorce. It is worth being able to experience the incredible joy that bringing new life into this world in the form of a beautiful baby girl brings. It is worth being able to love and be loved. It is worth being able to feel free.

> *"For many, the pain of our past creeps into our daily lives. Pain not adequately dealt with or worked through warps our ability to live in the freedom God has for us in Christ."*
>
> ~JAN FRANK, DOOR OF HOPE

How has abuse shaped the way you relate to others?

ADDICTION CHOKES INTIMACY

BEN

Addicts confuse intensity with intimacy. They say things like "we were closer in one night than I experienced in ten years of my previous relationship," and "I know we've only been dating two weeks but everything feels so right, so I'm moving in." These comments illustrate intensity not intimacy.

One key ingredient in developing healthy intimacy is time. Addicts don't like to wait; they want a magic bullet to feel better immediately not intentional intimacy over time.

I got drunk for the first time when I was 13. I got drunk for the last time when I was 28. In between, I quit a million times; but just because I quit getting drunk doesn't mean I quit being an addict. Addiction goes far deeper than using a substance.

One of my favorite books on addiction is by an alcoholic ex-priest, William Crisman, who wrote *The Opposite of Everything is True.* Many addicts feel their story is beyond all others in drama, pain and sometimes recovery. Crisman says, "The more extraordinary the story, the more ordinary the drunk." There are common themes for all addicts.

Crisman on the impact of his addiction said, "What I came to know with dreaded familiarity, though, is the inner stuff of chemical dependency - the feelings of isolation and emptiness, the cynicism of drained and empty dreams, the slowly-increasing paranoia, the quietly corrosive resentments, the compulsive need to be right, the unspoken but oh-so-real realization of being trapped and enslaved, and most of all the growing fear that I was going insane."

Isolation, emptiness, shattered dreams, paranoia, resentments, the demand to be right, feeling trapped and fear of being insane are not the foundational elements of intimacy, as you can imagine. Add other toxic tendencies like denial, justification, minimization, rationalization and lying to the traits of an addict, too. These don't help with trust and intimacy either.

All of this was underneath my drinking. I lived it all out in pathetic, self-destructive ways. I didn't know how to be close to Ann. When I quit getting drunk and was finally sober, I still didn't know how to be intimate emotionally. Without the facade of the buzz, I was exposed in my shame of not believing I was worthy of being loved.

Intimacy fills one's inner world with relationship with a person or persons instead of chemicals. Sobriety creates a base where growth can occur and where isolation transforms into connection through honesty. An addict may never totally eliminate a sense of emptiness but there can be an experience of others near you in your emptiness. Paranoia is replaced with safety and trust. Wounds are grieved, and conflict is addressed in a healthy, open way. Good conflict includes focusing on the problem and not the person; and it includes the hurt, why it is a problem and what would you'd like to do about it. The demand to be right becomes a genuine curiosity about the views and feelings of others. Being trapped morphs into a wide-open vista of life as an abundance of daily choices. The fear of going insane melts into an ability to love oneself and to receive love from others.

So intimacy is characterized by honesty, safety, trust, respect and value for the other. In our affair recovery these values grew in our marriage. We talked often, eye-to-eye, about our expectations, hurts, joys and dreams. We eventually sat closer and touched tenderly. I learned not to touch Ann so much on her boobs and butt so she would feel valued for more than her body parts. We had fun and played more, enjoying each other's presence. Spiritually we talked more about our relationship with God and encounters we had with Him through reading, church or small ways He caught our attention during the day. Sex became a place to give, enjoy and be enjoyed rather than perform. We journeyed into grace. It was a long journey, full of steps forward and steps back. We continue taking steps on this journey today toward deeper intimacy.

So by all means, get sober but know that is just the beginning. It's the beginning of the deeper soul work of owning all the dreadful ways you've treated others, entering the shame that fueled the addiction and discovering grace that has the capacity to melt shame. Grace allows us to be honest with our feelings about ourselves. Grace allows us to open up to the spouse who somewhere inside longs to be close. Grace creates space for honesty, and honesty is essential because without it the relationship is a mirage and intimacy a dream on the other side of the dune.

So give yourself and grace some time. Time to grow. Time to heal.

Are you addicted to alcohol, drugs, Internet gaming, porn, TV or something else? Reflect on the damage it causes to your own soul and the soul of your spouse. Humble yourself, get some help and find freedom.

KILLING MY HEART

ANN

*A*uthor Paulo Coelho recently tweeted, "The first symptom of the process of killing our dreams is when we say: 'I'm very busy now.'" The dreams for a deeply rich emotional connection in marriage are no exception. Without unhurried time together, intimacy will not be built.

I counseled a couple who said they wanted to work on their marriage. They were setting aside a little time to see me. They worked opposite shifts and rarely saw one another. When I suggested they eventually shift their schedules to build closeness, neither was willing to budge. "Oh yeah, ...um, right. That, uh, that is a good idea. But you see..." I understand that sometimes working opposite shifts (or long hours) for a time can be necessary, but this couple really didn't want to put in the effort to build closeness.

As we said earlier, we chose to reduce the busyness of our whole family after the affair came out. We limited our kids' activities to one hobby at a time. No more running from gymnastics to piano to basketball to Girl Scouts.

eight months, I took a job working Friday, ̣̣̣̣̣ and Sunday nights. I felt like a stay-at-home mom with the benefit of a paycheck. I could spend more unhurried time with our kids and spend time at their school. I could just enjoy who they are as our blessings. This schedule freed me up to have more time with Ben in the mornings before he left for work. I felt refreshed when he got home because I hadn't been working all day and running the kids all evening.

My new schedule allowed me unhurried time with God. I recovered a sense of who I really was as His beloved daughter. I had time to just sit with Him. Time to listen. All this made for a less-frantic, less-chaotic Ann. This conveyed to Ben that I valued him and our relationship as I was able to sit with him and listen to him. As a result, our hearts connected in intimate ways that hadn't been possible when I rushed around like a caffeine-crazed squirrel.

The Chinese pictograph for the word busy is telling. There are two symbols for busy: heart is one, killing is the other.

I was killing my own heart with all the busyness in my world. Slowing down, learning to rest and be still restored life to my heart and to our relationship.

What are you willing to remove from your schedule to have unhurried time with your spouse?

GHOSTS
IN THE BEDROOM

BEN

*"Issues that we have in general, we will also have
sexually. No technique or method will change that."*
~PATRICK CARNES

Sex with another man or woman is a thundering
tempest to the soul of a marriage. This violation
assaults a foundation of trust and rips apart
walls of safety leaving gaping holes. What once felt
permanent is suddenly exposed as vulnerable by the
jagged light and bass rumblings of the revelation of
an affair.

In one way, the revelation carries real trauma for
both in the marriage. For Ann, the exposure of her
betrayal cracked the denial she carried; she convinced
herself the affair would only minimally affect our
marriage. However, I received the revelation as an
ultrasonic blow shattering my illusion of a somewhat
idyllic relationship.

In another way, the revelation exposes truth. The
betrayal existed for a while; the lies were not new.
The affair partner didn't just appear the moment of

the revelation. Issues with closeness and intimacy impacted the relationship for a while. As Carnes says, those issues - those wounds and walls and fears - impact the sexual aspect of the relationship, too, which is now laced with the trauma of the revelation.

Couples respond in a variety of ways to the chaos of affair recovery. No right or wrong answer exists as to how much sex to have, if any, following an affair. Striving to learn the meaning of sex to each spouse and what it has meant in the marriage becomes key to eventually developing healthy sexuality.

Some couples enjoy sex often after the revelation. They may not have hopped in the sack naked this much in years. Perhaps it is a reaction of the betrayed spouse trying to hang onto the spouse or an attempt to measure up to the affair partner in some perceived standard.

Other couples have little to no sex. I've read that about 15 percent of all marriages are sexless. The thought of being *that* vulnerable with someone who just imparted a brutal wound is inconceivable to some.

Virtually, all couples will deal with the ghost of the affair partner. For the longest time, I sensed his presence in our bed. The truth wasn't that I couldn't enjoy sex with Ann. I did. God created sex to feel good. Still, the haunting sense of Ann's affair partner hovered around our marriage bed. I lamented: "How long, O Lord, will this go on? How long until the vapor of his presence will disappear from my enjoyment with my bride? Will this persist the rest of my days? How long, O Lord?"

Of course, there was no answer to how long. The ghost of the affair partner appeared and disappeared.

It seemingly departed and then stealthily returned, sending us back down a chute after climbing up so many ladders. After a while, I mostly dealt with this unwelcomed presence on my own. Discussing it only served to stir shame for Ann.

Ann and I had experienced much healing before we attended a conference together on the West Coast. When we arrived, I realized most of their encounters took place at this particular chain of hotels. The betrayal emerged fresh. The ghost showed up instantly like Spock and Kirk transporting from the Enterprise to a targeted planet.

But all those ladders gained were not lost. We had really done the work on our wounds, walls and fears; so tumbling down this chute didn't negate all that work. We just didn't foresee this challenge. We recaptured lost ground through a vulnerable discussion of our feelings, desires and commitment.

How long, O Lord? For you, I can't say. But I do know that understanding the issues you have in general, as an individual and as a couple, and understanding how those issues play out in your sexual relationship is a significant factor in the healing and growth and enjoyment of your sexual relationship.

What general relationship issues have you uncovered, and how do they relate to your sexual relationship?

PLAYFULNESS

BEN

Most relationships begin with a lot of play. Think back to your dating days. What fun times did you spend together? Ann and I watched and played sports. We enjoyed great food. We took walks. We just hung out with each other. Fast forward through our dating years to six years into our marriage with two kids. In trying to be a good Christian man, I decided that all our spare time would be family time. This sounded good at the time, but the decision left a deep part of my wife's heart neglected. Ann and I lost that sense of enjoyment and fun with one another that connected our hearts in the past.

Our relationship became dull. Lots of good, kind, meaningful activities filled our hours, days and weeks. We had fun with others and fun with our kids, but we did not have fun together. Together we paid bills, taught Sunday school, fed the dog, watched TV, etc. Part of Ann's affair (and most affairs) was recapturing fun and a sense of life, even when contrary to what one knows to be true and right. The intoxication of feeling alive again overshadowed reasonable thinking. Ann desired to feel alive again in our marriage.

Her desire was good. The direction she chose to pursue it was not.

Before we figured out how to bring play back into our relationship - before we even knew we needed to - another man showed up with time to give and enticed Ann. They went to the park. They enjoyed great food (even if it was on the corporate expense account). They laughed together. They had no daily routine to bog them down. It was hard to realize that my wife was not only having sex with another man, but she was also having fun with him. I had the choice of whether to learn from the most painful experience of my life or to stay resentful.

Though not a linear process, I eventually chose to learn and understand the message the affair delivered about our marriage. Part of the message of Ann's affair included that Ann and I needed to play together. You and your spouse both need play. Life is meant to be lived fully with lots of laughter. Ann and I recaptured a sense of play even in the midst of our daily routines. We like to be goofy together. We spend time outside hiking, biking and walking. We tickle. We joke. We play in the sprinkler, really. We laugh at ourselves. We flirt...I like flirting with her.

Where have you lost play in your relationship? How can you recapture playing together?

TALK AND TALK
SOME MORE

BEN

Another challenge in the aftermath of an affair is getting to a place of hope in the relationship as vision for a close, fun, trusting relationship vacates the radar. I had a vision for what our relationship could be. I didn't think it was possible or within my power. Out of gratitude to God I committed to stay and work on the relationship toward that vision. I intentionally showed up and made myself available each day as best I could. My prayer was, "God, I really don't see a way to make it to the other side of this thing, but maybe you do. Help me have the courage to show up to see what you can do in me and us." In some ways, it was a prayer of intentionality; and God supplied the means to make the miracle happen in our marriage.

One of the means He provided was space for Ann and I to talk and talk and talk some more. No longer did we need to hold back and keep secrets. We began to share openly and honestly in ways we had never shared. Man, was it messy! Anger, pain, tears and snot were everywhere. It was beautiful.

We shared stories of our lives during our marriage and before. I never knew how hard the early years were for her. She felt abandoned as I floundered in life, lost in an alcoholic fog. I shared the pain that pounded in my soul each and every day. I ached, now knowing she was having the affair when I began seminary. We shared more often and more honestly than we had before. Our emotional intimacy skyrocketed even with all the tension in our home.

We became more curious about each other's inner worlds. The more Ann told me the more I realized I didn't know about her feelings and dreams and pain. There was much I didn't know about her even though we'd been together for 13 years. There was much I never told her but assumed she knew about me since it rattled around inside me every day. Not a good assumption. I learned to tell her what felt obvious to me.

We learned a key element to a dynamic relationship (instead of a static one): If we are always growing, there will always be something new to find out about one another! There is always more for me to learn and discover about Ann. God is infinite inside of us. Ponder that one for a bit. I submit to you that if you are bored with your spouse it has more to do with you than him or her. So share your inner world, be curious and talk and talk some more.

Plan a time where each of you shares your inner worlds with one another. Shoot for 30 minutes of uninterrupted time, realizing however long you take is a good start.

AND TALK HONESTLY

ANN

*A*s you talk, be honest. Ben and I shared other secrets that came to light after I revealed my affair. Ben had a couple of one night stands while we dated that he told me about previously; but there was a third relationship that went on for a semester or so that he concealed. Those secrets kept us from really connecting.

Secrets are like a watermelon you're holding while trying to hug. They prohibit closeness and connection.

It wasn't just those big secrets that were important. Honesty in the little day-to-day emotions was essential, too. I had become a good and frequent liar. Lies became second nature to me. I could lie about anything and make it seem true. Shifting from hiding beneath the lies to exposing myself with the truth challenged me, but I had to learn so we had a fighting chance. Ben helped by keeping me accountable for my lies. He confronted me on the little lies and the big lies and reminded me that we couldn't rebuild trust if I continued to be dishonest with any area of my life. Ben also helped by being honest, too, though it was indeed a process of growth for both of us.

Remember this pithy but profound saying: you can have honesty without intimacy, but you can't have intimacy without honesty. If you don't have the depth of relationship you desire, take stock and see how many ways you conceal truth from your spouse. Get rid of the watermelons between the two of you, and be intentional about not keeping secrets large or small.

Now I get that sometimes honesty feels unsafe. Perhaps conflict doesn't go well in your house. When conflict goes poorly, coming back just as open is scary. So learn to do conflict in a way that you are *for* one another. As you share your internal world remember that you are on the same team, the same side. It may not always feel this way right now, but the more you develop that mindset, that this is *our* deal not just his or her deal, the sooner you'll be emotionally intimate in ways that didn't seem possible at the chaotic genesis of this journey.

> "Here's what I want you to do: Tell the truth, the whole truth, when you speak.
> Do the right thing by one another"
> (Zechariah 8:16).

Ask yourself, what have you been hesitant to talk about? Why is that? What important events or emotions (past or present) are you hiding?

I CHOOSE US

BEN

*A*s I mentioned before, I made the decision early in our marriage to use spare time as family time. You would think a husband and wife jointly decide on such matters, but I made the decision on my own. I thought I was being a good family man. I did not foresee that we would lose play and fun in our relationship. My decision left Ann feeling unchosen and uncherished.

Since learning a woman's most important question (do you think I'm beautiful?), I realize now my decision delivered a strong message to Ann. No. Ann did not feel her beauty was pursued or courted or affirmed. Ouch, that hurts to write even today. In the movie, *Family Man*, one of the poignant lines throughout the film is "I choose us." This means I will sacrifice in my life for the sake of our marriage. Our relationship is more important to me than success or money or our address. I choose us.

I didn't choose us though it may have looked like it. I left Ann lonely. Out of my weakness as a man it was easier for me to relate to the athletic side of Ann. She can run fast, she can hoop, she looked good in gym shorts and a t-shirt, but not too good or soft or intimidating for me. As I mentioned before, I didn't know what to do with her when she dressed in a softer, feminine way. So I mostly neglected her basic question. I didn't seek to take her out and court and delight in her. I was more comfortable with her on the basketball court than courting her.

At her core, a woman wants to know each day that she is lovely inside and out. I took for granted that Ann knew that. To be honest, sometimes I didn't care if she knew it or not. I didn't want to take the time for it, and there was this woman at work . . .

I began to eat lunch with my co-worker, Patty. We talked a lot, and she shared about her marriage, which was poor. So was mine, I was just oblivious to how bad it was. As wrong as it could be, I began to seek to answer *her* question. I wanted her to know she was valued and beautiful even if she was already married to another man. I gave my heart to her and left Ann vulnerable and isolated. My own decision to make spare time always family time left Ann feeling unlovely and unloved; it left me feeling not respected and connected to Ann. That leads us to Ann's affair.

For me, Ann's affair felt like the opposite of being chosen. Feelings of worthlessness and rejection covered me. If you are experiencing these feelings now stay with it. They can change and be redeemed. Today I feel chosen by Ann.

Ann now makes an effort to move towards me. I feel special in her eyes. She cycles to spend time with me as I enjoy my favorite pastime. She touches me often on my shoulders and arms to show her appreciation of my physical strength but more so my inner strength. This is in contrast to the distorted disrespect I felt during the only-family time period. I know now that Ann accepts me for who I am, and I don't have to try to be super Christian or super smart or super anything. I can relax in her presence in full knowledge that she chooses me. She chooses us. And I choose her. I choose us. In order to experience being chosen, your masks must come off and you must relate from your true self. Remember, the false self has no soul. It can't give or receive love. That's why secrets are so devastating to a marriage. So put yourself out there - warts and glory. It's a big risk, I know. If you are chosen while living out this risk it will be real and healing and transforming.

If you can say this genuinely, look your spouse in the eye, right now. Say, "I choose you. I choose us." If you'd like to say it but just aren't there right now tell them that. Honesty is better than faking an exercise just for the sake of doing it.

SOUL CONNECTION

ANN

*D*escribing God's work in the core of our soul is sometimes like trying to fork some pudding. Suffice it to say, spiritual intimacy is challenging for many.

Investment legend and spiritual development author John Templeton says, "No human has yet grasped one percent of what can be known about spiritual realities." We will never know all there is to know about God or ourselves. We are not only physical beings but are also spiritual beings. Remember, we may have been made from dust, but we are also created in His image.

As spiritual beings, our relationship with God is our most intimate relationship whether we are aware of it or not. Given that, if an overflow of that relationship isn't pouring into the marriage, there will be a huge chasm between husband and wife. Let's talk about how to bridge that gap.

An essential element of connecting spiritually is to respect and accept the different ways you connect with God. Ben likes to take a walk alone in the woods, and I like to hang out with 200 of my closest friends in the church lobby after service. If we're not careful, we can begin to look suspiciously at each other wondering, "Do you really love Jesus? Because you're just not doing it right."

These differences provide a wonderful means of living out the gospel and getting to know God more deeply. Being curious about why a certain discipline or soul training is helpful for your spouse - though it seems peculiar to you - can provide a means of spiritual bonding in the presence of broad differences. Accept and respect your spouse's *odd* ways. Also look for ways you can connect with one another spiritually doing activities together; we've listed a few ideas for you.

Read scripture together, but don't stop there. After reading, share the impact of the verses on your soul. Do the same after sharing a devotion or passage from another book for the same connecting effect between each of you and with God. I love it when Ben reads to me with his soothing and sometimes crackly voice. We then linger over what he's just read, absorbing the words and emotions into our souls. I recently read Ben a selection from a book I'm reading. The author talked about "embodying scripture." She relays an exercise she used with workshop participants to bring the Beatitudes to life without using any words. Her description of this process resonated deeply in my soul, and as I read to Ben my voice was the one that became soft and crackly as tears rolled down my cheeks. I let him in on what the Creator of the universe was revealing to and in me in those moments, and a beautiful connection between the two of us transpired.

Pray together. Praying from the passionate places inside of us feels so vulnerable. Because it is. Being vulnerable is a key ingredient of intimacy. Consequently, praying together from the depths of your soul will bring you closer to your spouse. Share what you need prayer for and ask the same of your spouse. Some days, this might be as simple as asking for a safe commute to and from work. Other days, it might be more complex like asking for strength to just lift your head off of the pillow and put one foot in front of the other. I ask for both from Ben, the simple and the complex. When I know that he prays for me, even if we're not together while praying, my heart connects to his in a soul-soothing way.

Worship together. In our culture, worship is often a euphemism for music at church. This is a sad reduction of a vast realm. Sometimes we worship to music in our kitchen or in the car. I have been found in my car with hands raised and liquid grace streaming down my cheeks on more than one occasion. Though worshipping through music enriches the soul, it certainly isn't the only way to lift our hearts to God. Going to church together certainly means worship, but go beyond just sitting in the pew. Begin to engage with the message after the service as an excursion into the depths of your soul that can be shared. Be curious about what was touched in your own soul and that of your spouse.

Enjoy creation. Creation leads to a place of awe and certainly points to our Creator. I truly am on the lookout for the beauty of creation when we walk together, whether it's wildflowers or the gnarled branches of a dead tree. As I share my observations of that beauty with Ben, we are able to stop and connect not only with one another but with the Creator of that beauty.

Share a ministry. Something happens in our hearts as we do Kingdom work together. Our souls become fertile ground for connection as we feed the homeless, wash dishes for the annual Christmas tea, teach God's word, lead others into His presence through groups and counseling and a million other ways to serve. Find just one of those million ways and begin serving together, and see what happens in your hearts.

Take a retreat, whether it is together or on your own. (Remember, individual growth is also an important part of this process.) Time away with no distractions is good not only for your connection with God but also with one another. After Ben's big leap of forgiveness toward me, we took a retreat to a lake house. Just the two of us and the fishies in the lake. We experienced an extraordinary connection of heart and soul as we relaxed on the couch, walked on the shore and read aloud to one another with no TV, no phones and no radio to disrupt that connection.

Simply talking about life and God grows spiritual intimacy. Be sure to have a listening ear and heart as your spouse shares from this vulnerable area. Any moment can be a spiritually-intimate moment. Remember, we are created in His image. We have the capacity to seek holiness in each other's hearts in any situation, in any moment. Seek and you shall find.

What are some ways you can contribute to soul connection with your spouse?

SANCTUARY

ANN

We have a porch swing given to us by my father who passed away three days after he turned 61. Too young, I know. That swing quickly became a favored sanctuary of mine. I nap on the cushions my mom fashioned out of cloth and foam. I marvel at the mountains I see through the trees from my front porch. God visits me often on that wood and reminds me that I am his beloved daughter. Ben occasionally joins me on the swing to share a meal in the crisp evening air or just to breathe the same air.

Ben created a *no-tech* zone in our living room. It is simply a corner with a chair, table, lamp, his glasses and books. He is the bibliophile of the family. He frequently stacks books on most of the horizontal surfaces of our home while devouring their words. But this corner is not only a reading nook. It allows space for Ben to connect with God. Not distracted by his phone, computer or Facebook, his soul is wholly available to God. I love when I find him here, lost in the love our Savior has for him. Sometimes he invites me to sit with him. I enjoy feeling the warmth of his heart while hearing what God has revealed to him when he's cloistered himself with Him. Then, with my head resting on Ben's leg, his hand gently resting on my head, I feel connected not only to Ben but also to God.

Sanctuary. Find it. Cultivate it. Share it.

Where are sanctuaries in your home? If there are none, where can you create one?

BRINGING
SENSUALITY BACK

BEN

I grew up in Columbia, Missouri. Interestingly enough, my hometown was once considered as a location for the filming of *Animal House*. Sadly, the chancellor at the University of Missouri didn't think it would reflect well on our university so she passed on the opportunity. Oh well. Nobody really remembers where it was filmed now anyway. I'm guessing Oregon.

I mention *Animal House* because for the longest time my understanding of sensuality consisted of the banter between Otter and Mrs. Wormer while standing by the cucumbers in a grocery store. Mrs. Wormer gave Otter an impromptu lesson about the difference between sensuous and sensual. She claimed vegetables were sensuous, and people were sensual. The banter occurred just before they engaged in an extramarital affair. At times, we are prone to ignore our senses. Then all of a sudden our sensuality gets rediscovered and enjoyed in the non-bill paying, non-laundry doing, non-childcare world of an affair.

To enrich your intimacy, bring sensuality back into your marriage. According to the American Heritage Dictionary, the meaning of sensual is "Relating to or affecting any of the senses." You know the five senses: taste, sight, smell, hearing, touch.

Being sensual is an important part of who we are as men and women, though we're often so distracted that our senses are seemingly disembodied in an alternate universe on someone's fingernail. (That's another *Animal House* reference, in case you are wondering.)

In his book *Sexual Anorexia*, Patrick Carnes, a renowned expert on sexuality, says, "In our culture, many people tune out much of what they're sensing. We're generally so focused on the task at hand that we miss most of what's happening around us...we simply don't pay attention . . . sensuousness requires stopping and paying attention."

Though it can be amatory, sensuality does not have to be connected with sexuality. It may be vitally important at this stage of your healing that you cultivate non-sexual intimacy which is all about developing the five senses without sexual involvement. And since sensuality is experiential, we suggest that you take some time to stop, pay attention and experience all of your senses as a couple. Enjoy a great meal together. Stop and smell the roses, literally. Hold hands. Listen to one another. Really look at one another. While this may feel uncomfortable to you in this moment, stay with it and allow yourself to be fully immersed in your five senses.

"If we're so busy that we can't pay attention to ourselves and the world around us – to be sensual in other words – we won't notice our partner either."

~PATRICK CARNES

Engage in one of the activities in the final paragraph above or create an activity you will both enjoy.

TOUCH, TRUST
AND MASSAGE

ANN

The Rocky Mountain Foothills made a stunning location for our church retreat. We were at breakfast in a rustic cafeteria with our friend, Norm. After eating, we enjoyed pleasant conversation. I leaned into Ben, and he began to gently touch my hair and scalp. I leaned in more. Ben took the cue and began to massage more purposefully. I closed my eyes and leaned in even more. My shoulders and arms went limp as I rolled my head around to make sure he didn't miss a spot. I softly cooed my approval.

Norm had been taking all of this in. When Ben finished my ecstasy of a scalp massage, I slumped into the chair in full relaxation, my hair looking like a 50-mph wind had roared through the dining hall.

Norm said, "Ann, do you need a cigarette?"

We all laughed long and loud. I laughed so hard I couldn't catch my breath for a few minutes.

This is just one example of how non-sexual touch can feel as pleasurable, in a different way, as sexual touch.

Before kids arrived on the scene we had plenty of non-sexual touch, but our non-sexual intimacy gradually disappeared. I felt whenever Ben touched me that he only wanted sex. I told him I felt like a thing rather than a person. In my longing for touch and connection, I would reach out to him. My heart shriveled when I extended my hand to his, and he jerked his hand away.

Now, massage enhances non-sexual physical intimacy in our relationship. We've relearned to communicate through nurturing touch. Massage is physical connection that encourages trust and understanding. It is an easy way to release physical tension, improve communication and develop a deeper, more intimate relationship.

Instead of reflecting on a question, I want you to get some lotion. Put some in your spouse's hand. Massage each of your spouse's hands for one full minute. Then switch and have your spouse massage your hands. Again, massage for one full minute each hand. This may be more intimate touch than you have experienced in a while. If you become sexually aroused during this time keep it in check, and make no sexual jokes during the exercise either. The focus here is on non-sexual intimacy. Enjoy the sensitivity and pleasure that God intended when He created you.

RECONNECTING AND RESTING
WITH THE TOP DOWN

BEN

One Sunday afternoon Ann and I went for a convertible ride. It was a beautiful summer day in the 80s and perfect for a ride, but at the start of the ride we weren't so connected or restful. You see, Ann had worked and attended a bridal shower. When she wasn't home when I expected her I texted her that I was going for a ride with the top down. I must confess I didn't have a great attitude toward Ann at the moment.

I was only about eight miles out when she texted back to say she was headed home. Though I didn't want to, I dug deep and asked if she'd like to join me. She said yes, so I turned the car around to get her. She was just about to settle in for a nap when I arrived home. Off we went.

We chatted some but mostly it was forced surface talk. Gradually, we began to relax, and the tension subsided. A big shift happened when I reached over to hold her hand. At first her engagement ring stabbed me. Perhaps I deserved it.

We initially shared about our day but gradually began to share more about our feelings, experiencing emotional intimacy. We felt closer as the arid, disappointing cornfields passed by on one side and the verdant green soy beans zizzed by on the other.

For us, the sights and smells of rural Missouri touch our souls. There are memories of visits to grandparents, other special farms and Ann's family land in southern Missouri. Recreation can foster a spiritual connection even as we merely tool down the road.

When I suggest engaging in recreation with your spouse, I'm not talking about a work hard/play hard concept. A lack of rest is often one of the precursors to an affair or other blowout. Sharing fun activities becomes a great way to rest our spirits and bodies and rejuvenate our relationships.

On our ride, we eventually relaxed and enjoyed one another's presence. We began to joke about sights we saw, enjoyed puppies by the road, told stories to one another and waved at Sam when we passed him on his afternoon bike ride.

I felt rested and recharged. I literally exhaled as we turned into the driveway. The exhale conveyed that the ride was exactly what I needed.

Isaiah 58:13 says the Sabbath is to be a day of delight, joy and celebration.

Recreation doesn't always have to be on the Sabbath, but suspending business as usual to enjoy life, each other and God applies to both recreation and Sabbath. A convertible ride provided a great lesson for me that day.

Plan a restful Sabbath activity with your spouse on any day of the week.

WILL I EVER BE ABLE TO FORGIVE YOU?

This question haunted me for 14 months with Ann. "Will I ever be able to forgive you?" At first I said I forgave her, but I was just trying to be a good Christian boy. I didn't really. Shoot, I didn't even know all of the ways she had wounded me. How could I forgive a wound I didn't even know I had? But in some circles that is the norm: forgive and deny the pain. It's a hoax!

I wanted to forgive. I craved the release I imagined forgiving would bring. So I learned another truth on this journey, forgiveness and grief are not the same. I was eventually able to forgive Ann, yet losses still needed to be grieved. Understand, I was never able to forgive in my own power. It came supernaturally.

Forgiveness came when I was able to own all God forgave me for. I owned my sins. It felt so unfair at first. I resisted. She had the affair! But in God's economy, our sins are about equal. None of us come close to being God. Jesus' words, forgive as I've forgiven you, persistently tapped me on the shoulder until one day the fullness of His grace overcame me. I melted into God through tears and snot, resting in his Grace and knowing that His love didn't fear my sin. He accepted all of me. I passed that Grace onto Ann. "I forgive you. We're going to make it."

FRIENDS IN THE TRENCHES

BEN

"We rejoice in our sufferings because we know that suffering produces perseverance, perseverance character, and character hope. And hope does not disappoint us because God has poured out his love into our hearts by the Holy Spirit whom He has given us" (Romans 5:3-5 NIV).

If you would have quoted this verse to me during the earlier times of our affair recovery, I think I would have punched you in the nose. I did not like suffering. I did not like persevering. Persevering is pregnant pain, and we lived smack in the middle of pregnant pain.

The grief and struggle was intense for me. I entertained every conceivable method of pain relief. Yet, I also desired to avoid additional future pain that unwise pain relief brings with it. There was a constant cage match rattling my insides.

We had many great friends support us in our struggle, but two men were pivotal for me, Sonny and Steve.

I trusted my Army Reserves chaplain, Steve Smallwood. I had drill the first weekend after I found out about the affair. I told Steve I needed to talk to him. We walked 30 yards down the hall, through the door and outside. Before I said a word, he looked at me and said, "What happened? Did your wife have an affair?"

Steve read it on my face. He had just been through the whole restoration process with a friend of his at church who had an affair. God placed him in my life. Without him, I don't know what would have happened. He really guided us.

He took me out to lunch that first day. He said, "Ben, your marriage isn't over yet, and God isn't through using you." I had thought they were both done. I didn't really believe him at the time, but I put those two thoughts in my back pocket. His words provided me hope during some of the deepest moments of despair.

Sonny was a friend at church whose daughter died in a car wreck injuring other family members. The tragedy of her death left Sonny with a deep understanding of pain. His pain was different but the depth familiar. We both had gas lines catch flame and blow up our worlds.

I could tell Sonny how I was feeling. I told him about a mirror I smashed with a 3 iron. He told me about going into his bedroom closet and kicking a hole in the wall. We both knew that sometimes we just needed to release some of the energy from the anger within. We connected that way and were honest with one another. I shared moments and thoughts with him that I didn't with anyone else.

Sonny invited me to Promise Keepers at the Texas Stadium. I told him I'd think about it. I didn't really want to go to a rah-rah event for God. Yet, I took the time off from work. I thought maybe I'd take another woman on a secret vacation if he didn't get back with me. (I told you Mixed Martial Arts was going on inside me.)

Eventually, the date drew near, and I didn't have another woman to take on vacation. It sounded so cliché when Sonny said, "We've got one more seat on the bus." *One more seat, Billy Graham.*

I drove the two hours to get my one seat, and we headed to Dallas. I wasn't in the mood to get all caught up in the hoopla, yet Pastor Tony Evans called men out. He used references from *Rocky 5* and the ghost of Mick, Rocky's deceased trainer, to tell us to "get up ya bums! The world needs men to get out of the gutter and fight." Pastor James Ryle also spoke. He focused on our desperate need for the Spirit. I grew a little more interested.

That night, Sonny and I went to the motel and I relived college days with pizza and SportsCenter.

At the end of the next morning, author and speaker John Maxwell spoke. He put three chairs on stage and told a story of three generations of men. One chair represented a man hot for God; the second chair represented his son who is lukewarm for God. The final chair symbolized the grandson who is cold for God. I began to stir and think about what I wanted to pass to my son, Payne. The battle inside felt like a tug of war between God and Satan. Did I want to go back to drinking and partying and get divorced? Did I want to continue on a path with God clinging to Him?

A guy came out in the afternoon to make announcements. They don't typically have altar calls on Saturdays at Promise Keepers, but he said, "I sense a lot of you guys are stirred up. We're going to have a time where you can come down if you want." Men streamed down the stadium. Thousands of men. Near the end, my tears were flowing, snot was rolling. As I got to the stairs, it was as though they went flat like in a cartoon, and I slid down to the floor. My pastor followed me down and asked me what was going on. I told him more than anything I just wanted to be close to God.

Fourteen months after the affair - after a ride home in my one seat on the bus and a two-hour car drive - I told my wife I forgave her.

Sonny and Steve were instrumental in walking with me through my suffering, my grieving, my disorientation. These great friends showed me much grace and constantly led me into the presence of Grace. Their love reminded me of the depth of Grace extended to me. I was privileged to be a conduit of this Grace to Ann.

Ann and I had moved from suffering and through perseverance. Pregnant pain birthed character, and I grew as a man. I also experienced hope seeing that God's Grace is bigger than any sin. Rev. C. Welton Gaddy says, "Grace fears no sin." We learned the startling truth of this statement and embrace it to this day.

For what has God forgiven you? Where do you feel you need forgiveness?

NAILS

BEN

A critical point of my journey into Grace came when God reminded me how blind I can be to my own sin and the depth of His Grace. He revealed this truth to me when I journaled a story titled *Nails*.

I wrote from my anger, which at the time felt righteous. I was sober and attending seminary to become a pastor. I turned my life around and pursued dreams for God. I perceived I was doing rather well following Him, and then wooooosh! I was pinned to the wall by a thousand nails with my arms spread out. Can you hear me identifying with Christ? About halfway through the story, God tapped me on the shoulder to expose my arrogance and self-righteousness. "Ben, we need to talk about a relationship you have."

He said, "The relationship with the woman (Patty) you've been close to at work isn't honoring to your marriage. Your relationship with her is a problem."

I hadn't perceived my relationship to Patty as a problem, partly because the desire passed to have sex with her. "That was close, but no harm done," I rationalized. God began to show me that wasn't really true. I caused much harm to Ann's soul because I was giving my heart to this other woman. (Jokes about a work spouse aren't funny when you understand the core wounds they inflict.)

Actually, a couple of months before I found out about Ann's affair I had decided to end contact with Patty. We hadn't been close for a while but would touch base every couple months. One day she called to tell me her husband filed for divorce. Soon after, Ann revealed her affair.

What a set up for me! Could this be God arranging for me to leave Ann in order to be with Patty? (Don't be fooled. God does not work that way.) Her voice became a powerful drug to me in my pain.

Our counselor helped me see the dynamics in the other relationship and bring it to a close. In all honesty, I did relapse with a couple of calls and emails, which I told Ann about. We finally labeled my relationship with Patty as an emotional affair. Emotional affairs devastate a marriage just as much as a physical affair. I left Ann lonely, abandoned and emotionally vulnerable. I was called to own my share of that and how I hurt Ann.

With my emotional affair there wasn't a trail of lies to deal with. I didn't lie to Ann about my whereabouts or whom I was with. My deception was mostly with myself. We did eventually talk through my emotional affair. I admitted my sin. I owned the damage I caused Ann's soul and asked her forgiveness.

What about *Nails*? Well, it's half finished and will remain that way. What began as my story to remind God of all the good things I was doing for Him and the gross unfairness of Ann's affair became something much different. *Nails* serves as a poignant reminder of the depth of my arrogance, blindness, hubris and desperate need for God's Grace.

Like me, has your arrogance been exposed in little or big ways on this journey? How so?

CRAVE GRACE

ANN

Forgiveness. Grace. Both include givers and receivers. Both involve letting go. Forgiveness requires a look at sin, our own or of those who have wounded us. Grace requires something much different. Grace requires looking to God.

I didn't feel worthy of forgiveness or Grace, but I received both from Ben and God.

The depth of Ben's forgiveness reflected the depth of his pain. His was not a shallow forgiveness. Forgiveness offered prior to an awareness of all the wounds received brings danger years later as those unknown wounds continue to bleed the soul dry. Ben allowed his soul to fill with the pain of all the stabs and gashes my affair brought that were then painted through with forgiveness. He knew the wounds that needed forgiving and in time he did just that.

Not to lessen the importance or impact of forgiveness, but Grace is so stunningly unexpected it creates an almost crippling sense of love. Crippling in a good way. Crippling in a way that brings us to our knees. Unable to move. Unable to utter a sound. Unable to resist.

During my healing I began to be still and quiet. As I surrendered a shift happened deep in my soul. An awareness surfaced of how desperate I was for Grace, even though I didn't feel worthy. None of us are worthy, but that's the whole point of Grace. We aren't worthy but God offers it anyway because He loves us that much. Little by little, I allowed Grace and forgiveness to become the lens of love I saw myself through, the lens of love I saw others through. It allowed me to believe that I could live a redeemed life. A life full of Grace.

I've since learned that Grace is about receiving from God and then pouring the same on others. In a women's group I led, we talked of Grace. We admitted how crappy we are at offering Grace to ourselves and to other people. It was a rich conversation, and made me crave even more Grace. Grace for myself. Grace for others.

"So these days I'm on the lookout for grace, and I'm especially on the lookout for ways that I withhold grace from myself and from other people," says Shauna Niequist, author of *Bittersweet.*

Tell the story about a time that Grace brought you to tears or stunned you into silence? If that hasn't happened, be curious about it.

HEALING GRACE

BEN AND ANN

*F*orgiveness through Grace can be tough to receive. In *Les Miserables*, Jean Valjean was rendered stupefied by it at first. As the story progressed, Grace began to radiate from him to others. He opened himself to God. Jean Valjean dared to live as a forgiven man. I encourage you to dare to live as a forgiven child of God. Allow healing to enter your soul.

The healing peace of Grace is a delivery from bondage. Though I {Ann} felt delivered, I felt as though a knife still protruded from my stomach. Receiving forgiveness from Ben helped heal me as it enabled me to begin to still my soul. In order to receive Grace, we must be still and stay in the pain. This seems counterintuitive. Won't accepting Grace be warm and fuzzy and peaceful all the time? The short answer is no.

In her book, Welcome to My Country, psychologist Lauren Slater shares the irony of first being a patient in a mental health facility and later returning as a therapist. Earlier we shared her profound words about stillness in her healing journey, "...health does not mean making the pains go away. I don't believe they ever go away. I have not healed so much as learned to sit still and wait while pain does its dancing work, trying not to panic or twist in ways that makes the blades tear deeper, finally infecting the wounds."

Even with the knife still in my stomach, when I am in my deepest pain, sometimes all I can do is sit still in front of God. There is no pleading, or praying, no twisting, just falling to my knees and being loved by my Father. In those moments, hopes of getting out of pain and restoring my marriage took a back seat where they rightly belonged so I could merely allow myself to be present with and loved by my God.

Healing for me {Ben} was a transformation of my relationship with God. I heard in my church circles that we were a once-saved-always-saved church. I believe God's Grace is outlandish and scandalous and beyond what we can imagine. If we are in His hand for a moment we are ever in His hand.

But the overemphasis of this thought led me to be passive in my faith to where I didn't surrender to God's pursuit daily. I can read Scripture and my heart still not be open to God. I have learned I need to have heart and soul time daily with Jesus. I need Jesus in the form of daily Grace tenderizing my soul.

I don't always remember, but I seek to remember, that without Grace I don't even take my next breath. Without God I just disintegrate. I fall apart. So as I learned to daily receive Grace I had a greater capacity to let God's love flow through me, like a cascade of water through a saturated sponge. Grace flowed through us, to restore our relationship, to develop more intimacy in our lives.

Like Jean Valjean, we were stupefied by God's Grace. In the shadow of our internal worlds disbelief initially reigned; yet throughout the months of recovery we surrendered more to His love. In overcoming our wounds and fears we dared believe that God's Grace was for us, and we dared to live as a forgiven husband and wife.

Meditate on the words above. What words or thoughts tug at your heart?

DISINTEGRATING DANDELION SEEDS

BEN AND ANN

"*I* will shrink or be less if I forgive." Does this fear ring true for you? This skewed thinking translates into "the offense didn't matter" as in "my heart and soul really don't matter."

What I {Ben} discovered during my 14-month journey of forgiveness was the opposite. The offense mattered and the wounds to my heart and soul did, too. I wrestled with a deep desire to punish in retribution. (Ann will tell you this became a reality at times with my sharp tongue). I longed to be free of the pain and pondered the illusion of peace through divorce. I ignored my own need for the Grace of God. Though I envisioned a way through, I was fogged in with the psalmist saying, how long will this go on?

About 13 months into recovery I attended a training with two coworkers. While there, we watched some pornographic movies in our hotel rooms. We also went to a topless bar where we took turns buying one another lap dances. None of this is prescriptive

239

by the way. I do not advocate this behavior. My point is God can and does pour Grace everywhere I go.

While the woman danced on my lap we chatted. I enjoyed the closeness with her. The skin on her shoulder was soft. At that moment, I understood how Ann could persist in her affair.

Later on I felt fallen. My inner residence lowered to knee high on a rat in the gutter of Scumbag Street. I was getting back in touch with my real condition. I'm not worthy to be loved by God, yet He chooses to love me with all of who He is. At the same time - with faith in Him - I can love with abandon and His Grace can flow through me to others in my life, even to a wife who made me a cuckold for three years.

God continued to illuminate the depth of my sin and the glory of His light within me. Six weeks after that trip I was eventually able to allow that Grace to fully go through me to Ann. I learned through all of this that it takes faith to offer grace, and as you offer grace, your faith grows.

Offering grace to Ann did not diminish me in the least. God grew my soul by allowing me to hurt over the betrayal, allowing me to grieve over the depth of sin in my own actions and more subtly in my own heart. My heart grew lighter after extending grace. Ann's did too.

God is about something bigger than my comfort. Trusting Him is essential in offering Grace. It is scary to trust God. Once I trusted God, the illusion of control disintegrated in the wind like white dandelion seeds drifting into the unknown. When we trust God, we are called to give up our right to revenge and instead offer His Grace to others. Forgive us our trespasses as we forgive those who trespass against us. That's

Matthew 6:11-12, and it can be an excruciating passage to live out fully.

Much of the time I {Ann} wasn't sure we'd make it. Sometimes my heart puffed up, and I took on an arrogant attitude that Ben could do what he wanted. He worked in a town about 50 miles away and talked of getting an apartment there, living there most of the week and coming home on weekends. I didn't have the best response in my heart to this possible new development. I thought, "I don't need him; I can make it on my own. If he's doing this to see if I can do it on my own, well, I'll show him a thing or two, cause I know I can do it on my own." Put a little head bobbing in there, and you'll get the attitude just about right. Not a very grace-ful reaction, eh?

I'm grateful that God sees deeper than that - to the more true part of me, to the part humbled by the thought of His Grace coming toward me even when I have those black thoughts. His Grace did come. Ben did not move 50 miles away. My heart was softened. By Grace. I am ever grateful that it was and ever grateful that not only my heart was softened but so was Ben's.

We shared this earlier from Harry Schaumburg, but it bears repeating: "Faith should be defined as knowing that He sees us in the chaos." Even if you are not feeling his Grace, it is still coming towards you.

We were often confused in the pain and disruption of our lives. At times it was difficult to see where God was or even if He was. He is. He says call me I AM. I AM always moves toward us with Grace. Always.

What aspects of your marriage or of the affair are you not ready to forgive?

JUST AS I AM

BEN

As we moved through recovery, Ann and I experienced a deep level of gratitude. We realized we never would have made this journey of our own choosing. We were deeply humbled before and with God.

Author Brennan Manning says, "It takes a profound conversion to accept that God is relentlessly tender and compassionate toward us just as we are, not in spite of our sins and faults (that would not be total acceptance) but with them."

That was a new thought: He loved all of me. I didn't need to cover myself up; God wants to be with me just as I am. It's no surprise to Him that I'm not perfect.

I heard a sermon once that mentioned a huge part of Christian maturity is recognizing just how subtly - and not so subtly - we are sinful and self-centered. We recognize overt sin fairly easily; but recognizing our subtle self-centeredness allows us to more fully receive the abundance of God's Grace. We also begin to grasp His acceptance of us as *who we are* right now, not for what *we can do* for Him.

God's acceptance is always there. Ann and I owned our despicable self-centeredness (not in a self-contemptuous way but in an honest, grief-filled, humbling way). Allowing His acceptance to drive us to our knees opened our eyes to the profound depths of His Love. We rest in being chosen by Him.

He delights in glorious and wretched Ben and Ann. We are grateful for His delight.

"But God demonstrated his own love for us in this: While we were still sinners, Christ died for us" (Romans 5:8).

What are you grateful for in your life? Write out a list with everything big and small.

THE LEAST OF THESE

ANN

God delights in us, even with all the junk we bring. Easy to say, but tough to experience. This journey helped us experience more of His delight.

As I read Brennan Manning's book, *Ruthless Trust,* I began to further own my core identity as Abba's Child.

Imagine yourself approaching the Creator of the universe. What is your posture? Are you running, arms flailing and head thrown back? Are you hiding, like a child in trouble, unsure that He even wants you there? Are you walking steadily toward Him, sure that He loves you? Are you crawling, barely able to utter a sound as you pull yourself toward Him with every fiber of your soul, completely spent by the time you reach Him?

Now, imagine yourself reclining in Abba's lap. Imagine being held and rocked as you converse with Abba. Can you see it? Can you feel it? Can you sense His delight as He embraces you and gazes on you lovingly?

Knowing I am delighted in gives me the security and freedom to face the pain in my life, to enter the messy process of life like restoring my marriage. If I live with Abba's child as my core identity, I begin to taste the freedom and glory of being His child.

I spent the three years of my affair *appearing* to be in the posture of running toward God with all that I had. I was the superstar volunteer at church. We were baptized in May, and by August we were teaching Sunday school to three-year olds. Soon after, we began helping with the youth group. I joined the choir. I helped out at every potluck, and as Baptists, we had lots of potlucks. Essentially, we were at church every time the doors were open. The only problem was that in reality I was running *away* from Him as fast and as far as I possibly could.

I was nowhere near His lap.

I was like the younger prodigal son in Luke 15 who was in the far country, nowhere near home OR the father. Then the son came to his senses. He started the journey home thinking he would just be one of his father's servants since he didn't feel worthy to be his son anymore. While he was a long way off, the father saw him. In a shameful act in his culture, he hiked up his robes baring his legs and sprinted to his lost son. When the father got to him, he kissed his face. The verb tense doesn't denote a single kiss. It implies that the father kissed his son's face again and again. He couldn't stop kissing his son with delight and love at his return.

Imagine the Father sees you and sprints to you. Visualize him kissing your face with excitement and tenderness.

I seldom felt worthy to receive His kisses. Is it tough for you to imagine God kissing your face tenderly too? Matthew 25:40 says, "Whatever you did for one of the least of these brothers of mine, you did for me." Who do you consider as one of the least of these? Stop and get an image, a face in your mind.

Have you ever in your life stopped to ponder...

What if the least of these is...ME?

Now as one of the least of these imagine the Father kissing your face again. He can't stop kissing you because He loves you that much. Allow yourself to lean into His tenderness and drink in His delight of you as His beloved daughter or son.

Take five minutes. Imagine God holding you in His lap or kissing your face. What is this experience like for you?

HE DOESN'T CAST US OUT

BEN

"Ben, your marriage is not restored. Once your wife cheated on you, you have no marriage. It's over. It is a terrible thing to continue the charade. Turn her out and get a decent woman who will be faithful. You are just fooling yourself and playing a dishonest game. She is no good and deserves the worst. You are acting like a fool. The Almighty has a decent woman out there for you. Just have the courage to look."

When I received this email I was ticked off! I wanted to tell him where to stick it! Then God helped use my anger to lead me further inward to greater depths. In those depths I experienced closeness with God in a reassuring personal way. Rather than lashing out in a similar graceless manner to the sender of this email I penned the following response acknowledging the truth that we non-Jews are grafted into this whole scandalous grace-filled Gospel.

Aye, she did cheat on me, and it hurt tremendously. I am well acquainted with the feelings of why adultery was punishable by death in the Old Testament. When

I found out about her affair, God showed me some of His heart in that law.

God also showed me other aspects of who He is. He showed me that I too deserved to be turned out. I was let into this party undeserved myself. I was a drunk. I missed my son's first birthday getting drunk at a golf course. I blasphemed. I didn't provide for my family. I lived a coward's life *then*.

I could fill up an entire blog of why I do not deserve this gracious love of Father.

And Father does love me. He does value me as His son. I am dearly beloved. Today, I try to live from the strength and courage He has filled me with. He showed me some of it when I called out to Him and quit drinking a few months later. He showed me more in dealing with the pain of adultery.

The foolish thing would have been to cut and run when I found out about the affair. The act of a coward would have been to send her out and to seek another woman. But God showed me that the woman with the Scarlet A is sometimes the most righteous woman in town. I saw God churn and soften my beloved's heart. I witnessed a miracle in her heart and in my own. The Almighty, because He has chosen her and because she abides in Him, has made her a decent woman. Nay, she is not a decent woman. She is a beautiful and glorious woman. She is the bride of my youth. Father delights in her and sings over her. So do I.

This Kingdom Journey is not all about me. I do not claim to have the perseverance of Hosea. But I know something of His walk. If I thought only of what brought me the least pain in the moment I would have sent her out. I would have missed out on what God really means for marriage. I would not know the joy that He has set for us in this life between husband and wife. Suffering does really produce perseverance, and perseverance really does produce character, and character really does produce hope. Hope in Him. I walked with the bride of my youth through the Valley of Achor, and we both entered into His Hope.

My Lord and Savior did not send women out. He castigated the men who thought themselves worthy of doing so. He chastised the ones who said, "Thank God I am not like the sinner." He treated the hearts of women like treasures of great value instead of viewing women as a mere possession.

Jesus encountered the adulterous woman. He took his time. He played in the dirt for a while. He stood up and talked to the men who wanted to stone her, and then he played in the dirt some more. He did not stone her. And then he offered her great words of hope. He conveyed to her that she was not her worst behavior. She was more than a woman who slept around. She could leave that life of sin and be more.

My Ann is more. Yes, she did sleep around. She is more. The pain of her sin has been used by God to make her even more beautiful and glorious. It is Father's great gift to me that I am permitted to be her husband.

What words of discouragement have you received about your marriage? Ponder deeply, how would you like to respond to them in the future?

ENCOUNTERING GOD'S GRACE

ANN

The Lord your God is with you.

No matter what you think, He is with you. Many have asked, "Where was He when . . .?" Abuse, tragedy, trauma, death - especially premature death - are all situations that cause this question to bubble in our souls. And the revelation of an affair certainly feels tragic, traumatic and nearly like death.

Even when you don't pay attention to Him . . .
The Lord your God is with you.
Even when you don't feel Him . . .
The Lord your God is with you.
Even when you question His presence . . .
The Lord your God is with you.
Even when you can't take it any more . . .
The Lord your God is with you.
Even when you feel another tear can't possibly
fall from your lashes . . .
The Lord your God is with you.

Hear this if you hear nothing else . . . The Lord your God is with you.

He is present in the friendships that renew your soul. My friends, Krista and Jenn, they listen and laugh with me. Our mood together is unhurried as we linger with the essence of our souls.

He is present in the images of beauty that stir your heart to seek more. Like the morning when I caught a glimpse of the sun rising in the distance. I chased off down the street in order to get a closer glimpse. I ended up sitting in my car in the middle of the parking lot (not in a parking spot mind you, truly in the middle) for a good 10 minutes watching the sunrise.

He is present in the warmth of the sunshine as I sit in the café courtyard all alone enjoying my leftovers for lunch.

He is present in the phone call made to my friend whose mom is dying. I am sad for my friend because she will miss her mom but a little jealous of her mom that she has now gone to meet Jesus.

He is present in the stillness of the quiet morning as I sit in my antique rocker snuggled in my ladybug blanket soaking in His word and seeking His Grace for the day.

Again, hear this if you hear nothing else . . . *The Lord your God is with you.*

Read this reflection a few more times. Rest in the mood and words.

EVIL DOESN'T
GET THE LAST WORD

BEN

*I*t really was that bad. It really was wrong.

Forgiving does not mean we take the edge off of the evil done to us. Wrong is wrong. Ann's choice to have an affair was wrong. It was sin. Owning that evil helped me in several ways.

First, naming her sin helped me to own my own sin and evil in the relationship. I made calls to another woman; I emailed the words "I love you" and wrote an occasional card to this other woman – all of which I concealed from Ann. Even though I had become sober I was able to own how difficult my drinking made the early years of our relationship. Owning the *wrong* of her actions also helped me to more fully own the subtle self-centeredness I battle with every day.

More so, calling her affair wrong gave me permission to explore it beyond just being wrong. It allowed me to see how her choice to have an affair was understandable. I saw her good desires for affection and fun, her family history of sexual sin, her history of sexual abuse, the ways I hurt her heart and how all that set the stage for the affair. Her story didn't make her choices less evil; it made her choices understandable. When a choice becomes understandable, it becomes more easily forgivable.

Finally, owning the evil helped to deepen the meaning of my forgiveness. Because we didn't smooth things over and minimize the evil in her deception, we both experienced freedom when I forgave. Though our sin is really *that* bad, God's grace for each of us is really *that* big; and we are able to pass it on to one another.

My eyes opened. Understanding myself as betrayed and Ann as betrayer applied to just one aspect of our marriage. Ann lied to me and cheated on me. But in other areas of our marriage, I was the betrayer. As I explored Ann's story I saw beyond my pain to who she was as a wounded daughter of God. Neither of us had any idea how much our past wounds influenced our present relationship and choices.

When it came to a deep, sincere forgiveness of the wounds she caused me, I looked Evil square in the face. I told Evil that he doesn't get the last word in my marriage. As I forgave Ann for the wounds and pain she caused me, chains clanked to the ground and we were both set free.

What are you both learning that is making the affair more understandable?

FORGIVE AND REMEMBER

BEN

Forgiveness is easier to accept when you recall how much God has forgiven you.

Matthew 18 tells the story of a servant who owed the king $100,000. The king forgave the debt. The servant then went to a man who owed him $10. The man couldn't pay so the servant had him thrown in jail. God is like that with us, forgiving us our millions that we could never repay. He acknowledges our debt, forgives it and showers us with His love. Yet, often we fail to remember His forgiveness, usually when we are wounded by others.

I can be so petty with my wife sometimes. I am wiser now so I don't speak my shallow complaints as much as before, but I still battle that urge. She may say something or do something that ever so slightly misses my heart, and I feel the fury rise within. The anger feels so real, and I feel so justified in the moment.

Later, God usually comes to me slowly and tenderly. "Ben, my son, let's talk. Tell me your story." I tell all the painful pieces. "I'm not happy you drank until you couldn't walk or were suicidal, but I really dig that part where you called out to Me. I cleaned the slate and take joy in holding you close."

I am then able to see Ann through different eyes. My heart softens, and if we need to talk we do; but most of the time I merely put my hand on her shoulder or gently stroke her cheek or kiss her forehead.

Through remembering God's Love in forgiving all of my sins and selfishness, I am closer to Him and closer to my wife. Forgiving does not mean that we forget what happened. It's absurd to think one would ever forget a spouse's affair and all the emotions that come with betrayal. Jan Frank says in *A Door of Hope*, "The challenge is not to forgive and forget. The real honor comes in one's ability to forgive and yet remember."

Forgiveness means more when the fullness of my sin and the fullness of my wounds are faced and remembered.

Spend time in prayer about your story. Where do you experience God's delight?

FORGIVENESS
DOES NOT EQUAL TRUST

BEN

Forgiving does not mean that we invite someone who hurt us once to hurt us again.

Don't confuse forgiveness and trust. For your own benefit it is essential that eventually you forgive the betrayer. Forgiving does not mean you immediately trust this person with all of who you are. He may not be trustworthy - yet. When trust is broken the betrayer must earn trust to restore it.

With infidelity recovery, I often see the one who strayed demand to be trusted right away or soon after. Often this demand includes some subtle spiritual manipulation, "You said you forgive me so you should trust me if that is really true. If you really forgave me you wouldn't doubt that I'm telling the truth."

These statements are a form of manipulation because he or she just acted in a non-trustworthy manner. The damage that is done - lies, sex outside of marriage, sometimes significant amounts of money spent – are all part of the betrayal. These take a significant amount of time to recover from even though forgiveness may be granted for wounds before all the damage is healed. Whether a person transforms from one who can't be trusted to one who can is still to be determined.

So trust and forgiveness are two different animals. Forgiveness is for the one betrayed to eventually offer to the one who strayed. Pray into that. Seek to understand your wounds, feel them and offer forgiveness.

Trust is for the one who strayed to *earn* through long-term consistency and consideration for the feelings and desires of the one who was betrayed. Ask your spouse or partner what he or she needs from you to help rebuild trust. Some typical responses include: being accountable for your time and whereabouts, ending all contact with the affair partner and disclosing if any accidental encounters occur, and reflection on your part seeking to understand your story and why you were vulnerable to an affair. Having a non-defensive attitude about questions and conversations also illustrates your openness and willingness to tend to the soul of your mate. Compassion for the pain you caused will help facilitate the granting of forgiveness and trust, though these will most likely occur at different times.

Our hope remains that you both experience healing, which includes an abundance of forgiveness and trust.

Where are you and your spouse in the process of forgiveness and rebuilding trust?

GLORIOUS RUIN

BEN

"80 percent of what we see when we look at a person who recently wronged and deeply wounded us must lie behind our eyes in the memory of our pain. We filter the image of our villain through the gauze of our wounded memories, and in the process we alter his reality."

'THE ART OF FORGIVING' BY LEWIS SMEDES.

Following the discovery of Ann's affair, I saw her as the wrong she did to me. Mostly what I saw when I looked at her was a dark wall of pain mixed with red hot streaks of anger. When I didn't see that, I saw only a liar and adulterer holding a knife dripping with my blood. The gauze of my wounded memories distorted the image of who Ann really was.

Before the revelation, I knew she wasn't perfect. She could be short with the kids or me occasionally. She could have a tough time saying no and get overcommitted and overinvolved with a bunch of worthwhile projects. A little gossip slipped out here and there about a co-worker or friend at church. But infidelity, cheating, sex with another man? No, no, no. She would never go there. An affair? Nope, she's not capable of *that*.

She certainly was and is. So am I. So are you, and so is your spouse. Every person on this planet is capable of heinous self-centeredness. Initially, through that gauze of wounds, all I saw when I looked at her was a betrayer.

I saw Ann through a different lens before I found out about the affair. I saw her through a view that was more about how she made me feel. I wanted her to be who made me feel the best. I wanted her to be always happy, always glad to be with me, always pretty so that life would be easy. I wanted her to be my Easy Button. That's not love. That's me attaching a hose to her and sucking the life from her into me.

Through these faulty lenses at first I saw only what made me feel better. Then I saw only what hurt like hell. Moving through forgiveness meant dropping the lenses and getting a clear picture of Ann's humanity.

Slowly, I began to see the way I either idealized or villainized Ann. She was either just about Jesus or just about Satan. I had placed her in the impossible place of being responsible for everything good in my life or responsible for all the pain. She lived in my *either/or* split screen of good and evil.

Ultimately, a clearer lens to view Ann developed for me. A lens of *both/and*.

I began to accept that Ann was woman, a human. She possessed a wonderful heart, capable of blessing others in tremendously self-sacrificing ways. She was a woman with a dark side, capable of serving her own desires and needs while locking away an awareness of the long-term consequences to those who love her most.

As I write this I don't for a second forget that I'm the same way. That's in fact my point. Slowly, I began to see and experience that we share a common bond in our humanity. Much is written about the differences of the sexes. In truth, we are far more alike in our humanity than different in our gender. In our marriage, we were both amazingly kind and shockingly selfish.

I began to see in her a glorious ruin. Glorious ruin is a phrase borrowed from C.S. Lewis. We are glorious in that we are made in God's image. Really. Ponder that a bit. Let it sink in. Ann is made in the image of the Creator of the universe. And she is a ruin that is marred and disfigured but not so much that the original image disappears.

She is a human in need of a savior. Just. Like. Me. I need a savior, too. Just. Like. Her.

Both of you make a list of the way you are glorious and you are a ruin. Read your lists to one another. Affirm the vulnerability of your spouse in making such a list.

MODEST MIRACLES

BEN

Once you see your spouse's humanity and give up on vengeance you may actually begin to desire some good for the one who caused your pain. In other words, you will become okay when God grants some Grace to the betrayer. It isn't a strong feeling at first, but it builds and eventually you will feel sincere in being glad for God's kindness to the betrayer.

Looking back, a war exploded within me. At first, it seemed the enemy would win. Hatred, anger and bitterness had the upper hand just like two boys alternating hands on a baseball bat until they get to the top, and the last hand to grasp the bat gets to pick first. Hatred, anger and bitterness picked first and batted first. And they hit hard!

But they didn't account for the conversations that took place before they really hit. I remember telling Ann, "We'll get through this. It won't always look like we will, but we will." I told my daughter, Stephanie, "I'm really mad at your mom, but we'll stay together. We won't get divorced."

I didn't always believe those words, but they were there, in the dugout so to speak. They fueled the late inning rally of forgiveness along with the early words from my chaplain, Steve Smallwood. "Ben, your marriage isn't over, and God isn't through using you."

Over the course of 14 months (roughly 444 days), hatred, anger and bitterness were outscored by love, sorrow and compassion. Her affair hurt like hell but became understandable to me. I saw where I, too, needed grace. God's Grace flowed through me and I offered grace to the bride of my youth. He was way ahead of me. In this I can be sure that I was teamed with God in a modest miracle of healing.

Spend some time in prayer asking for your marriage to be part of a modest miracle of healing.

FORGIVE THROUGH ME

BEN

I felt searing shame that I was unable to forgive completely for more than a year. On one hand, I wasn't going to fake forgiveness. It had to be real to me or I didn't want to offer it. On the other hand, I'd read verses like Colossians 3:13: "Be even tempered, content with second place, quick to forgive an offense. Forgive as quickly and completely as the Master forgave you." I felt hopeless and powerless when I read this passage.

I felt like a failure when I thought about forgiving in my own power. Forgiving my wife all the wounds from three years of lies and sex with another man was beyond my capabilities. I was trying to do that on my own, and it was too big.

Renowned theologian Dallas Willard generalized the first three steps of the 12 steps of recovery:

I admit that I am powerless over sin and that my life has become unmanageable.

I believe that God - through His action and those of His Son Jesus and the Holy Spirit - can restore me to sanity.

I will turn my will and my entire life over to the care of God.

Life had become unmanageable. Check. Believing that God could restore me to sanity, sometimes I forgot that, though I had experienced that in my own life when I called out to God as a drunken, broken-down 28 year old. Done. Turning my will and life over to God . . . that was a quotidian battle.

For 14 months I prayed. I didn't realize how much prayer I was actually doing. "I'm mad at you, God. I don't trust you," is a form of prayer. "Cuss word, cuss word, cuss word," can be a form of prayer, too. Romans 8:26 says, "Meanwhile the moment we get tired in the waiting, God's Spirit stays right alongside helping us along. If we don't know how or what to pray, it doesn't matter. He does our praying in and for us, making prayer out of our wordless sighs and aching groans and cuss words."

Okay, forgive me. I added the cuss word part, but I see the cuss words as part of my aching groans, part of my prayer, part of my life psalm of lament.

Fourteen months is a long time to fight this battle. But if I see my marriage as lasting 150 years like our friends Wes and Judy suggest, it's just a blip on the timeline.

So, I prayed. I learned not to pray for the strength to forgive. Sure, my will was certainly a choice in the matter. I prayed for the Lord to forgive through me. I prayed to join in with the forgiveness that God - and almost everyone else (which stirred up anger at first and later more shame) - was offering Ann. . . .

"Forgive through me. I can't do it on my own."

Notice the implicit trust in that statement. Forgive through me. It's acknowledging the power and truth in Steps 2 and 3. God, through His action and those of his Son and the Holy Spirit, can restore me to sanity. I'll turn my will and life over to Him.

I prayed this in a "Lord, I do believe; help me overcome my unbelief" way. Pray it I did. I prayed it until I slid down those stairs in Texas Stadium knowing that God was the best thing ever to happen in my life and more than anything else I wanted to be close to Him. Forgiveness happened at that moment in my heart. I rode the bus back to Springfield, drove home and shared that forgiveness with Ann.

Spend some time in prayer connecting with the Grace and Love of the Spirit. Offer up your aching groans and wordless sighs.

A VALUABLE
14 MONTHS OF HELL

BEN

Today was a wonderful day.

Good friends from Dallas came to visit. My family blessed me to overflowing. My wife procured some Lamar's doughnuts for breakfast, which are way better than Krispy Kreme by the way. She also gave me greens fees for two at a unique golf course. My son gave me a pound of good, dark, smoky coffee. My daughter gave me a new book by Paulo Coelho. For dinner, my wife grilled tender pork chops, fried potatoes, steamed broccoli and melted cheese to put over it, and we had salad. For dessert, we had vanilla ice cream with strawberries on top to tickle my taste buds. I am full, body and soul. Ann and I just returned from taking our dog for a walk around the lake while the mountains watched from afar.

It was really a great day.

Maybe you are wondering if your marriage is going to survive. People say you don't want to stay together just for the kids. I couldn't agree more. You don't. But they are a great reason to stay engaged in the affair recovery process with all of who you are. Grow and rebuild your marriage over the next few years together. Postponing the decision for a couple of years about whether to stay married or not takes pressure off of the recovery process.

It may be tough to face all of the pain you are in. What am I saying? It *IS* tough to face the pain of infidelity. I sincerely believe that if a man and a woman are willing to humble themselves, face the truth (all your glory and sin), face life head on daily and seek God (whatever that means during this chaotic time in your life), I can promise you it will be worth it. You will grow and be closer to God. This gives your marriage the best chance of surviving, and I promise you will be changed for the better.

So often, during the worst of times in our marriage, a huge part of me wanted to run and not face the pain. I am so glad I didn't heed that voice and had friends get in my way sometimes when I wanted to. If I had given into the pain I wouldn't have had the day I had today. This day would have been a mere dream and not a reality. Many times I only stayed for the kids. I stayed reluctantly, but I stayed. I grew and changed. Ann grew and changed. Today, we are together and really like each other. Really like each other. Ann is such a good friend and companion.

I am blessed for staying and facing the pain. Fourteen months of hell. Fourteen months of growth.

A couple of years of struggle and toil, humility and confession, anger and hurt have brought me to a place of joy I only dreamed of years ago in the midst of all the devastation. I pray that redemption and joy for you.

What dreams do you have for your future with your spouse?

WHERE DO WE GO FROM HERE?

Congratulations on making it three months with us! You may be wondering, now what? Where do we go from here?

In addition to all we've shared, we want to leave you with several guidelines as you move forward. We will provide you with some practical markers to check 90 days post-revelation. In this last section, we discuss how to handle birthdays, holidays and the one-year anniversary of the revelation. We share some key principles of restoration to underscore your efforts. A key in recovery for us was really learning to listen. We conclude with the story of a courageous couple who spent five healing days with us at a marriage intensive in the Rocky Mountains.

90 DAYS IN

BEN

a few summers ago, I pondered my first charity bike ride for MS. Until then, my longest was about 20 miles. Great encouragement came from my friend, Gary, who told me, "You don't have to ride 100 miles. You only have to ride 10 miles 10 times."

He was right. Every 10 miles or so there was a rest stop with all sorts of energy bars, peanut butter and jelly sandwiches, sports drink, water, bananas, orange juice and pickle juice (to prevent cramping).

After those first couple of 10 mile sets, it still felt like a long way home. When I thought about the entire ride I wasn't sure I would get there. I'd refocus. I brought my mind back to the present. "Just ride the next 10," I'd tell myself. One talks to himself a lot on long bike rides.

So, congratulations! You've made it three months! Seriously, congratulations. Many, many couples don't make it this far. One person may not want to try. One may not be willing to end the affair. One may get lost in the pain taking on a zombie aura. But you, you are here. Enjoy some refreshment. Take in some nourishment. Exhale. You've done good work so far.

Remember to watch out ahead. There are potholes, rainstorms, loose gravel, texting car drivers and giant hills. The cool thing about those hills...when you get to the top...the ride down is fun, exciting, thrilling. You'll just have to trust me. I've made the ride. It's worth the risk for the thrills you'll get the rest of your life.

You've made it three months, and that is terrific. Seriously, it is. This is hard, hard, hard stuff to go through.

Here are some practical markers to have hit by now. If not, keep moving towards them.

1 All contact with the affair partner has stopped. All.
2 Many in-depth conversations with your spouse about the marriage as a whole are taking place. There are still conversations about the affair, but the overall relationship is talked about more.
3 A shared definition of the meaning of the affair should be in process. The affair was a bad way to communicate to your spouse but still you were trying to say something. Ann was telling me that she wanted to be cherished and have more fun in our relationship. I was treating her more as a co-parent than a lifelong lover and companion. I had gotten too serious as a Christian.
4 You have one or two couples who are for your marriage and point you towards God. They can hang out and talk about the hard stuff or laugh and have fun. You can be a mess around these folks.
5 Have a counselor or pastor help process your losses. Experience this as a couple and individually.

6   My friend and mentor, Tom Varney, told me about three actions that help all couples. I've reworded them in alliterative form. Be intentional about these three L's:

1   *Lay down your sword* - Do your best to express your anger in a way that doesn't do more harm to the relationship.

2   *Look at your own stuff* - What did you contribute to the problems in the marriage?

3   *Listen* - Be curious about your spouse's soul.

Be obedient in blessing your spouse even if you don't feel like it. It's not fake-it-til-you-make-it. It's *I'm hurt, and my soul is bloody; but I choose to live from a deeper place in me that loves my spouse as I hang onto hope that God is transforming my heart and our relationship into one that delights Him and us.*

I'm glad you made it this far. I know it's hard and painful, and sometimes you feel like giving up. But you can do this. Be encouraged. Ride on. The rewards are worth it.

ARE SPECIAL DAYS STILL SPECIAL?

BEN

Holidays can be awkward. Just think of the last time you made small talk with a distant relative wearing too much perfume and ended the conversation with a clumsy hug. Holiday complexity increases when recovering from an affair. The tension in the air requires a different resolve when around other family.

That first Thanksgiving post revelation, Ann and I decided to avoid all that and instead spent four days apart.

I felt sad yet oddly refreshed with the days apart that first Thanksgiving. It was a mini separation, if you will. We generally don't advocate separation when dealing with an affair. Too many important conversations happen on the fly that may not happen if a couple lives apart. While difficult, living together requires interaction with one another. I believe in most cases it keeps the process moving.

I felt sadness from not having my wife by my side while I spent time at my parent's house. Ann spent time with her three siblings and other friends. Even though melancholy enveloped me, the 120-mile distance from her lifted me out of the large dark mass that was our marriage. It was an important time to decompress and reflect.

No right or wrong way exists to handle holidays, but do your best to be intentional about the situation. We spent Christmas together that year and hosted members of Ann's family. I didn't fake a celebratory mood, yet, I did my best not to be Debbie Downer. I survived and appreciated having guests in our home. Ann appreciated the sense of normalcy at Christmas. She relaxed in her element of cooking, laughing and being with others. The holiday represented a small step forward on our jagged journey.

While holidays bring a different element to your recovery so do birthdays, your wedding anniversary and the one-year anniversary of the revelation of the affair. Ann's birthday arrived a mere three weeks after the revelation. Nothing inside me wanted to celebrate her that day. However, I found a hope for the future within my soul. I realized my kids deserved to celebrate their mom. I brought home a cake and ice cream; we sang and celebrated Ann. Moments like this built hope for the future as we learned to live out the Gospel by blessing each other while in pain.

The first anniversary of the revelation may pass uneventfully or be a sucker punch in the gut. Ann and I experienced growth and hope for almost a year. As the anniversary approached, I pondered our lives a year prior. I believe it was then I realized we bought two houses while she carried on with her affair partner. New pain, new wounds. While Ann did nothing new to hurt me, my realization was new, so the wounds felt fresh. As much as I tried to anticipate the anniversary I didn't see this one coming. So be aware, new turbulence often emerges around this time. If you've stayed engaged throughout the process, you'll be able to regain forward momentum after a few unexpected bumps on the road.

Special days may not feel as special during recovery. Most likely the celebration will be different than typically experienced. Expect the unexpected as they approach. Know that emotions may swing back and forth like a high-speed pendulum. By maintaining your vision of the future, you'll be able to make decisions to love through the pain, building hope for the future.

KEY PRINCIPLES OF RESTORATION

BEN AND ANN

The world of restoration following an affair is a dangerous roller coaster ride. We've seen couples sure to make it ultimately file for divorce months later. We've seen couples poised with the cap off of the pen, ready to sign the divorce papers, celebrate their anniversary after a few sleeps. We can't predict who will or won't be able to find restoration and redemption following an affair. Yet, a few principles seem common to the couples that do survive and develop a better relationship. Keep in mind these are far from a guarantee with the slow rises, dramatic falls, hairpin turns and loopty loops contained in the emotional, spiritual and physical ride post affair revelation.

First, your relationship with God becomes central. This includes some deep honest wrestling full of doubts. Black and white areas become more gray, reducing all-or-nothing thinking. You will learn more of real relationship with God, which is more both/and rather than either/or thinking.

Also, your marriage becomes a primary priority. All decisions go through the lens of how it impacts your relationship. This includes avoiding people, places and activities that harm your marriage, copious amounts of time spent talking about your relationship past and present with no subject off limits, and participating in activities that reinforce your marriage. Each spouse develops an appreciation of the other's perspectives.

Next, both spouses commit to a full processing of the relationship. The decision whether to stay married or not may be put off but each spouse stays engaged in the messy processing of emotions and the marital story. An awareness of reconciliation prior to regaining total trust is evident. This means acting with kindness towards your spouse or partner before you really feel like it. It's not fake-it-til-you-make-it. It is acting in a way that acknowledges hope for the future even though hope may be just a small flicker of light at the moment.

As part of the full processing of the relationship, honesty and full disclosure are a must. Though initially more difficult, it is best to have all secrets disclosed in the beginning. Slowly revealing information over weeks or months throws the process backwards. The betrayed experiences a loss of trust and returns to step one.

Additionally, each of you needs to make a commitment to lifelong individual growth. Two dynamic individuals create a vibrant relationship. An old book by Charlie Jones described it as being "on the grow." Another description is learning to live a reflective life.

Finally, finding community - among families, friends, counselors, church - needs to happen. Your close friends are people who let you be where you are but who bring an awareness of God. They are present with you in the here and now, in your anger, cussing, frustration and sorrow; yet they bring transcendent reminders without pounding you over the head with God talk. These folks will be people you can genuinely laugh and cry with. They'll hang out with you and talk about your *stuff*. They also like to just hang out and enjoy Settlers of Catan, Reverse Charades or a game of cards.

Understand though that knowing these principles and going through a boatload of healing doesn't make us invulnerable to desert times again. As we travel through the desert we learn much about our journey, including where we experience freedom that leads to greater intimacy with God, with each other and with ourselves.

THE TEETER TOTTER OF RECOVERY

BEN

The time frame from about five to seven months post affair was brutal for me. I'm an American. I own a microwave oven. Stuff isn't supposed to take this long! I discovered my soul isn't a frozen pizza, and neither is yours.

Throughout the first 14 months - until a huge leap of forgiveness took place - part of me wanted out every day. It was especially hard around the six month mark. I felt trapped. The pain droned on inside me like an endless REO Speedwagon ballad. *I'm just gonna keep on tormentin' yoooooooouuuuuuuuuu.*

It had been six months for crying out loud (though sometimes not so out or loud). The crying came in many forms. I didn't think I could deal with it anymore. REO was on another verse, the flight response kicked in, and I called my lawyer friend, Matt, who was also a groomsman in our wedding.

There are risky moments in any affair recovery where the marriage balance teeters and totters. I was ready to bail out on my side and send Ann crashing to the ground. God had other ideas in having me call Matt.

"Hey Matt."

"Hey."

(Small talk)

"Ann's had an affair. We've been trying to work through it, but I'm done. Should I get a lawyer in K.C., or can you help me out?"

"Ben, maybe this is what you need to do. I deal with this stuff every day. Everyone thinks they'll go through it, and it won't be so bad. It's always harder than people imagine it will be. It starts off okay and then mistrust kicks in and anger; and then it just gets mean. And it hurts. It just rips people up. There is so much pain in divorce. *Ben, if there is any way, stay and keep working on it.*"

Matt spoke profound words of life to me when I desperately needed to hear them.

Here I am now. My wife of 30 years just gave me a big smooch. She is wonderful, and I'm glad we're married and stayed married and like being married to one another. I have no idea what my life would be if Matt hadn't been a great friend to me in that moment on the phone.

Are you tired of being in pain? Are you worn out and wondering if the pain will ever go away? It does hurt, and it hurts a lot. Of course part of you wants out, and divorce can seem like a decent option.

But if there is any way, stay and keep working on it. Eventually the pain can go away and joy can be restored in your relationship. Your marriage can be better than anything your imagination allows at the moment. But it's a slow cook deal. It can't be rushed.

So to God and Matt, thank you from the bottom of my heart. When I was about to make a great mistake you helped me glide down and gently touch the ground. I landed, looked up. I saw the bride of my youth who hurt me bad. Your words gave me the courage to gently push off skyward and keep the balance as we teetered and tottered along.

LISTEN, REALLY LISTEN

BEN

Any couple can have difficulty communicating because of inefficient conflict resolution skills. We were one of those couples. Good communication is more than learning to talk; it also means learning to listen well. Three words are important to remember when communicating: *intentional, curious* and *for*.

Good communication doesn't just happen. First, actively and intentionally seek out good communication and grow into it. Second, be curious about your spouse's soul. There are universes to explore in there. Finally, remember that you're on the same side. Be for the other person. (This can be tough sometimes in dealing with the anger of an affair but do your best to be on the same side as your spouse.)

Be *intentional*. Be *curious*. Be *for*.

We avoided conflict in the early years of our marriage. We were masters of the silent treatment. We swept our issues under a rug that gradually piled up to the ceiling. Conflict avoidance is a problem for many folks who were taught, above all, being Christian means being nice. We've learned to share what needs to be shared, in a timely and appropriate manner. In doing this, garbage doesn't build up under the rug.

Another helpful skill we learned was the Speaker/ Listener Technique from marriage researcher and author Scott Stanley and his book, *A Lasting Promise*. We highly recommend this book because the Speaker/ Listener Technique creates a safe environment so you can more clearly communicate with each other. Stress is as high as a Mariah Carey top-end note when healing from an affair. We still use this skill when stress is high.

When talking to Ann, I learned to express what was going on in me. I quit trying to tell her how she should think and feel. Through the early years this was quite invalidating to her soul. We both learned to express our inner worlds more clearly and non-defensively. One way we did this was to cease using *you always* or *you never* statements. Many situations are both/and and not either/or. Learning to accept some gray areas accelerated our healing.

Another helpful skill is to become aware of your mood as you enter a conversation. One acronym to remember is H.A.L.T. This stands for: Hungry, Angry, Lonely or Tired. Consider if you're experiencing hunger, anger, loneliness or need for sleep, then carefully evaluate if this is the best time to go deep in conversation. If all four are present, a rescheduled talk is definitely in order.

Most importantly, be aware of your own strategies of self-protection or masks. To some degree, we all fear that being close to another isn't safe. An affair certainly confirms that. Each one of us has a battle going on inside our soul. We want to be close, yet we fear being too close. In our fear we construct barriers to keep people away. These barriers include people pleasing, being tough, performing, being a party animal, overworking, busyness and others. As a result, the soul is protected by masks. When love hits a mask the wearer doesn't receive it, the mask does and love evaporates into the air. Do your best to be open and authentic with your spouse.

So what's the goal of good communication? In good communication the primary goal is not to determine who is right or wrong; it is to more fully know and understand one another. The goal is showing real respect and honor to one another, not agreement.

To realize this goal learn to listen well. Learning to listen, really listen, helped us know one another more deeply and move forward in our recovery.

EVERY FUCK IT IS WORTH A THOUSAND WORDS: AN INTENSIVE

BEN

"Fuck it! Fuck it! Fuck it! Just Fuck it!"

Thus began the third day of a marriage intensive with a tentatively hopeful couple. The husband started the morning with his F-bomb proclamation. I looked around to see if somebody in charge would know what to do. My face looked calm while my insides freaked as I realized the person in charge was me.

The intensive began earlier that week with Ann and I sharing our story and answering questions from the couple. On the second day, we taught on betrayal, grief, guilt and shame - you know, the lighter stuff to ease them in. They are given reflective exercises to ponder and encouraged to share their thoughts. We chiseled into some longstanding walls separating these two.

We were meeting at a vintage Rocky Mountain cabin. At the end of the second long day of the intensive, I felt tired as they left. It was a good tired, a hopeful tired. Then, on Friday morning, after enjoying the cool of the morning and peaceful gurgling of the backyard brook, the F-bombs snapped Ann and I out of our overconfidence.

For over a year, I met weekly with this man who had a hard story. Part of the difficulty was his denial of the hardships he faced as a boy. After charming the boy's mom his father charmed the world as a charismatic salesman. They moved thousands of miles away from family and support. Before the boy would carry his backpack onto a yellow bus to kindergarten, his dad bolted from the family. How does this type of abandonment pound the heart and soul of a little boy? Security and safety vanish. Innocence is lost. A world without mom and dad and a cocoon of love leaves the little caterpillar exposed to harsh elements before his butterfly wings form. He had no ability to fly through and above storms.

Mom was left with two small boys in an unfamiliar state. She leaned into her nonexistent friends and crashed to the ground. She drifted and numbed her pain with substances and younger men. The little boys grew into tweens with immature men - only a decade or so older - *guiding* their paths.

Once, he got into big trouble for stealing his mom's pot stash. The boyfriend of the time erupted spewing acidic shame. Nothing of substance about being a man was being passed down. He learned that he had to take care of himself; he couldn't count on the adults in his life, so he began to act accordingly.

Some older girls in the apartment complex enticed him into sex before he was in high school. At the time, this seems like such a thrilling triumph.

The damage goes unnoticed. Closeness and safety only happened during sex was the illusion being cemented. He carried this tilted view of life and love into marriage.

We tend to choose a companion at the same emotional level. This couple was no exception. This man and woman didn't realize the wounds and immaturity of their souls when they pronounced their vows of fidelity in perpetuity. Why would they? Life progressed in good order as a decent job allowed her to stay home with the kids.

But remember the myth that closeness and safety are only found during sex. The boy who carried this deception into manhood demanded more and more sex. The girl who carried her lack of solid womanhood (partly due to a demeaning mother) determined that she had no other course than to submit to his sexual demands.

She wore the color of underwear he wanted. Awoke at the time he wanted. Went to sleep when he wanted. She offered her body to him morning and evening, every day. Fourteen times a week they had sex. The man concluded he had hit the jackpot - his lotto numbers matched up. He had the wife of all wives and all the sex he wanted to support his myth. He was a real man. But like all idols, eventually this one falls in on itself after satisfying for a time.

The woman eventually shared her story to a newfound friend. The friend informed her that her husband was abusing her. After a time of gaining strength the woman left for a shelter. The man was pissed! Who did she think she was to leave him like this?

About this time I began meeting with him. He was angry at her, didn't want to look at his past ("I've left all that behind me") but also wanted her home. For a year they lived separately. She healed and grew stronger while he and I met with some progress in owning how he had hurt her. But deep inside he wanted things to go back the way they were.

He did grow but occasionally the myth broke through the surface. This husband voiced demands, but the wife now had the strength of NO. Fights ensued. Enough positive change occurred for her to move back home. We decided on a marriage intensive to power through what continued to snag their ankles as they reached for freedom.

Fuck it! Fuck it! Fuck it! Just fuck it!! He was stuck. He realized he could be an ass but didn't know what else to do. He still wanted lots of sex but also was tired of the stress around it. He knew his past ensnared him, but he hated to admit it. Then he screamed words of hope. "I don't know what else to do."

He was done scrambling, done trying to do it in his power. He found the end of his self-centered self. His myth shattered and crashed like a glass shower door. He put more trust in us and, most importantly, in God.

A month after the intensive the four of us met again. I saw a new man. He relaxed into the couch. Fear didn't control him. Instead of intensity, I saw security. He didn't need to prove himself or vigilantly scan the room to stay safe. He rested as a tender, strong man who was finally able to fly.

If you are interested in an intensive or video counseling, contact us at marriagesrestored.com.

A big desire in our lives is to share the hope we received from others when our marriage was on the line.

CPSIA information can be obtained
at www.ICGtesting.com
Printed in the USA
BVHW070633010321
601377BV00002B/111